Bitemporality in Go

Burke Carter

First Edition: February 2025

Published by Burke Carter

Library of Congress Control Number: 2025903203

The information provided is for educational purposes only and does not constitute professional advice. The author has endeavored to eliminate as many bugs as possible, but it is unlikely that they have all been squashed.

Foreword

Databases aren't magic, but they sometimes seem to be. From those that hold all of their data in only a single file on your local disk to those that store data on a network of machines that spans the globe, there seems to be a database for every niche. What they have in common is that in fractions of a second, a single record among millions – or even billions, or even more! – of others can be retrieved, modified, or even erased. During the process, other records – and even other queries – can be affected or unaffected depending on the guarantees of the software. I am endlessly fascinated by that software.

If you were to ask a contemporary software engineer to name a few types (not versions or vendors) of databases, you would probably hear a fairly consistent list: relational, NoSQL, key-value, or maybe even columnar. Missing from that list is the enormously clever model called the bitemporal model, which is arguably on a different axis than the others but is nevertheless just as important in its own domain. I would go so far as to argue that the bitemporal model is more distinct from the others than is row store from column store. It takes some time to learn to think bitemporally, but it's time well spent for the queries that can be so elegantly expressed this way.

Working on databases is great fun. I hope that you enjoy working on this one as much as I have.

Table of contents

Chapter 1: Why bitemporal data

Rarely is data static. Our knowledge of the world changes continuously, and we continuously make decisions based on that data. Different data compels us to make different decisions in the present, but that doesn't change the state of the world as we knew it in the past, nor does it change the decisions that we made at that time. In order to preserve the historical record and to understand why what now seems foolhardy was once reasonable, we need to maintain that history. This is the *raison d'être* of bitemporal data.

Let's illustrate what I mean with a simple example. Suppose that our HR application keeps track of employees and the department in which they work:

ID	First name	Last name	Department
1	Alice	Andrews	IT
2	Ben	Baker	Operations
3	Clara	Campbell	R&D

It would be easy enough in a relational model[1] to count how many employees work in each department:

```
SELECT department, COUNT(*)
FROM employees
GROUP BY department;
```

That's a perfectly good point-in-time snapshot. How about transferring an employee to a different department?

```
UPDATE employees
SET department = 'Operations'
WHERE id = 3;
```

That works, but it also causes data loss: we no longer know Clara's previous department! There are at least three cumbersome solutions to this problem:

- Keep both an `old_department` and a `current_department` field. This accurately tracks the first transfer an employee makes, but not the second (or the third, or ...) move. To track an arbitrary number of transfers, we would have to add an arbitrary number of columns.
- Keep `department` as a sorted list of the employee's history such that the first (or last) entry in the list is the employee's current department. This keeps the full history, but it is cumbersome to query and may require a very wide column if employees frequently change departments. For

completeness, one would probably also like the dates associated with each move, further expanding the column.

- Keep a "history table" with the employee's ID, their old department, the date of their transfer, and their new department. So long as the main employees table is kept in sync with the history table, this does not lose information. However, some queries, such as "which department had the most employees on date X?" become difficult to answer because the state of the world on date X must be carefully reconstructed from the history.

But there's an even worse problem with the third cumbersome solution above: what if the transfer was effective as-of date d_1 but was recorded on a later date d_2? Suddenly, it's not clear what is meant by X in "which department had the most employees on date X?" Do we mean to ask how many employees were effectively in the department on date X, or do we mean to ask how many employees were known to be in the department on date X? Perhaps it's not immediately obvious that this distinction matters. To see the significance, you need only imagine that if Clara's transfer to the Operations department would increase her salary, then she would certainly want the increase to begin on $d_1 < d_2$, perhaps requiring backpay that would be paid on d_2.

The right solution is to model this data bitemporally by assigning four extra fields to each piece of data:

Field	Significance
tt_from	When the data was first recorded by the database
tt_to	When the data was first invalidated by the database
vt_from	When the data became true in the real world
vt_to	When the data stopped being true in the real world

In our example, the tt_from would be d_2, since that's when Clara's transfer was recorded in the database, and the vt_from would be d_1, since that's when her transfer became effective in the real world. Both tt_to and vt_to are initially set to infinity since when we write a record, we don't know how (or even if) that record will change in the future. Note that while the vt_from is set by the user, the tt_from is always chosen by the database and is monotonically increasing so that history cannot be overwritten. As we'll see, even though data initially extends to infinity, we cannot read it after the lsqt, or "last safe query time," which is the latest time at which all writes have either completed or failed such that the data up to that time will never change. Together, these two rules mirror two principles of life: you cannot change the past, and you cannot see the future.

Graphically, the data exist in the bitemporal plane where the `tt`-axis is the x-axis and the `vt`-axis is the y-axis. On Clara's start date, her bitemporal space would look like this, with the * showing the `(tt, vt)` at which she began her career:

```
^ ^
| |
| |
| |
| |
| |
| | Rectangle 1
| | First name: Clara
| | Last name:  Campbell
| | Department: R&D
| *--------------------------------------------->
|
--------------------------------------------->
```

To record her transfer at **, rectangle 1 is split so that instead of its `tt` extending to infinity, it now extends only to Y. Rectangle 2 is created with the same data as rectangle 1, and it extends from `tt = Y` to `tt = infinity` with the same `vt_from` as rectangle 1 `vt_to = X`. Finally, rectangle 3 is created with the new data with both `tt_to = infinity` and `vt_to = infinity`.

```
  ^ ^                         ^
  | |                         | Rectangle 3
  | |                         | First name: Clara
  | |                         | Last name:  Campbell
  | |                         | Department: Operations
X | |                         **---------------------->
  | | Rectangle 1             | Rectangle 2
  | | First name: Clara       | First name: Clara
  | | Last name:  Campbell    | Last name:  Campbell
  | | Department: R&D         | Department: R&D
  | *--------------------------------------------->
  |
  --------------------------------------------->
                    Y
```

Now, we can ask questions like, "as of (* ≤ `tt` < Y, `vt` == X), what was Clara's department?" Restating this question, "at * ≤ `tt` < Y, what did we think was Clara's department starting at `vt` == X?" In the image above, we can see that these temporal coordinates fall inside the rectangle labeled 1, so the answer is the R&D department. If we were to modify the question slightly and ask, "at `tt` == Y, what did we think was Clara's department starting at * ≤ `vt` < X?" These temporal coordinates fall inside rectangle 2, so the answer is again the R&D

department. Finally, we can ask, "at `tt == Y`, what did we think was Clara's department starting at `vt == X`?" That falls inside rectangle 3, so the answer is the Operations department, the department to which Clara transferred.

Why this book

There are plenty of resources available that will tell you what bitemporality is, but until now, there has been no comprehensive guide to teach you how to build a database and client that inherently support bitemporality. By the end of this book, not only will you have a working knowledge of the core concepts, but also you will know how to program in that model, and you will have some ideas for additional features that you may want or need.

This book is structured as both a guide and an implementation. If you follow along, you'll implement a server and a client for a bitemporal object database. Throughout the book, you'll also read about alternatives that would provide different properties and trade-offs. It's up to you to decide how to extend the provided source code to match your specific use case. For brevity, most of the thousands of lines of tests are omitted from the book and exist only in the source code itself. Most of the non-test code appears in the book in short snippets with accompanying explanations. At times, the code is broken into shorter functions than usual in order to avoid functions longer than a single page. Likewise, the physical pages of a book are more narrow than a large monitor with an IDE, so some code that would appear on a single line in an IDE is broken into multiple lines.

Dependencies

The main dependency is Go, the programming language that we will use throughout this book. Its combination of clarity, performance, and ease-of-use make it the ideal language for this endeavor. To build a faster version, you could use Rust or C++, but as a language for teaching, Go wins with simplicity. Along the way, we will also use some open source libraries such as Protocol Buffers.

We'll use Go version 1.24.0, but we won't use any advanced features specifically from that release. A slightly older version should also work.

```
$ go version
go version go1.24.0 linux/amd64
```

 The most surprising dependency might be SQLite. This book is not about how to implement a storage engine, but rather how to implement a bitemporal database on top of your existing storage—after all, most projects already have a traditional or general-purpose database, and the piece that they're missing is bitemporality. Because of the architecture that we'll use, it would be possible after reading this book to swap the storage with, say, PostgreSQL, or any other storage of your choice.

We'll use SQLite version 3.49.0. As with our choice of Go version, we won't use any advanced features specifically from that release, so a slightly older version should also work.

```
$ sqlite3 --version
3.49.0 2025-02-06 11:55:18 \
  4a7dd425dc2a0e5082a9049c9b4a9d4f199a71583d014c24b4cfe276c5a77cde (64-bit)
```

 For hermetic builds, we'll use Bazel, and to make generating BUILD files easier, we'll use Gazelle.

We'll use a bazel version manager called bazelisk with version 1.18.0, bazel version 7.3.2, and gazelle version 0.35.0.

```
$ bazelisk version
Bazelisk version: v1.18.0

$ bazelisk --version
bazel 7.3.2

// WORKSPACE

http_archive(
    name = "bazel_gazelle",
    integrity = \
      "sha256-MpOL2hbmcABjA1R5Bj2dJMYO2o15/Uc5Vj9Q0zHLMgk=",
    urls = [
        "https://mirror.bazel.build/github.com/" + \
        "bazelbuild/bazel-gazelle/releases/download/" + \
        "v0.35.0/bazel-gazelle-v0.35.0.tar.gz",
        "https://github.com/bazelbuild/bazel-gazelle/" + \
        "releases/download/v0.35.0/" + \
        "bazel-gazelle-v0.35.0.tar.gz",
    ],
)
```

1. The examples in this book use vanilla SQL, but any similar query language should suffice. ↩

Chapter 2: Server API

```
// proto/server/reader/reader.proto

service Reader {
  rpc ReadLsqt(ReadLsqtRequest) returns (ReadLsqtResponse) {}
  rpc Read(ReadRequest) returns (ReadResponse) {}
}

// proto/server/writer/writer.proto

service Writer {
  rpc Write(WriteRequest) returns (WriteResponse) {}
}
```

The database API defines how we will access data, and many subsequent decisions will be based largely on what API we choose. Therefore, it's imperative that we choose a simple, well-defined API with well-defined behavior.

It is not important that our API supports every conceivable feature. Rather, the supported features must allow the user to interact with the data in a sensible way while leaving room for future improvements.

Objects

All objects stored in the database will be uniquely identified by an `ObjectId`, which will be a UUID by default. Users may implement their own function for generating the `ObjectId` if they wish, though it still must be unique within the database.

All objects must have an `Fqn`, or *fully-qualified name*. This is the import path followed by the identifier name in Go. In a language like Java, it's likely the class name.

All objects will be automatically indexed by their `ObjectId` and their `Fqn`. Objects may also define additional attributes to be indexed with varying levels of uniqueness. Some examples befitting a simple telephone book application are: a `LastName` field to quickly find 0 or more people by their last name at a given `(tt, vt)`; a `PhoneNumber` field to quickly find 0 or 1 people to whom that phone number is assigned at a given `(tt, vt)`; and a `RecordId` field that uniquely identifies a record in the database for all time.

Reads

Except for `READ_LSQT`, all reads happen at a `(tt, vt)`. This will become obvious when we get to Chapter 9 and implement the client.

`READ_LSQT` – get the latest `Lsqt`

  - Requires no arguments

`READ` – get zero or more objects by index(es)

  - Requires a `(tt, vt)` pair
  - Requires one or more index predicates

Writes

All writes happen at a `(tt, vt)`, but the user specifies only the `vt`. The `tt` is assigned by the database and is returned as part of the response to a successful write.

`PUT` – write one or more objects

- Requires a `vt`
- Requires one or more `BdObjectIs`
- Requires one or more `lastReads` for existing `ObjectIds`

`DELETE` – delete one or more objects

- Requires a `vt`
- Requires one or more `BdObjectIs`
- Requires one or more `lastReads`

`RESTORE` – write one or more objects as they were at previous `TemporalCoordinates` and maintain a link to the previous version(s)

- Requires a `vt`
- Requires one or more `BdObjectIs`
- Requires one or more `lastReads`

Wire format

If our database is to be generic, we must choose a wire format that allows many diverse clients to connect. For that reason, we choose Protocol Buffers, an industry standard for language agnostic data exchange.

Chapter 3: Server Modules

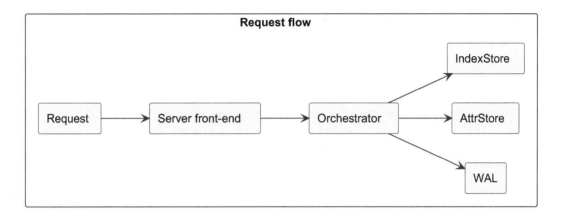

Request flow

Request → Server front-end → Orchestrator → IndexStore, AttrStore, WAL

Like any good software project, the database will be separated into modules with clean interfaces hiding implementations.

Server frontend

Clients will connect to this, and each client request will be automatically handled in a separate goroutine. In a production system, this is where we would add interceptors like authentication, rate limiting, and so forth. Our implementation has no-op authentication as a pointer to show where to add such things, but to keep the focus on the database itself, we will stop short of adding something more secure or sophisticated.

Orchestrator

In a design diagram of our system, this would be in the center, orchestrating the flow of data. It will make calls to the other modules and perform safety checks like preventing conflicting operations.

Write-Ahead Log (WAL)

This will log all operations prior to executing them in the database so that if an operation fails unexpectedly, we can roll forward or roll back.

Attr(ibute) store

This will store a JSON-serialized representation of the attributes of individual object instances. It won't know anything about the attributes, though—it will simply store bytes that will be interpreted elsewhere. Note that there's nothing special about JSON when it comes to bitemporality. Any reasonable serialization format would be suffice.

Index store

This will store the indexed attributes of the object instances. Entries in the `IndexStore` will reference entries in the `AttrStore`.

Client

This will allow users to connect to the database over gRPC.

Generator

This will generate code to make the client-side API more ergonomic. In particular, it will allow users to work with objects (`structs`) rather than writing raw gRPC requests.

Example

While not a part of the database, an end-to-end example will demonstrate the functionality that we have implemented.

Chapter 4: Server Frontend

```go
// server/main.go

type server struct {
  readerp.ReaderServer
  writerp.WriterServer
  orch *orchestrator.Orchestrator
}
```

The frontend is the home of the `main()` function, the beginning of every Go program. It will construct and start the gRPCserver and wait for cancellation, such as a termination signal. Let's look at the `server` first. All it will do is delegate to the `Orchestrator`.

```go
// server/main.go

func newServer(orch *orchestrator.Orchestrator) *server {
  return &server{
    orch: orch,
  }
}

func (s *server) ReadLsqt(
  ctx context.Context,
  r *readerp.ReadLsqtRequest,
) (*readerp.ReadLsqtResponse, error) {
  return s.orch.ReadLsqt(ctx, r), nil
}

func (s *server) Read(
  ctx context.Context,
  r *readerp.ReadRequest,
) (*readerp.ReadResponse, error) {
  return s.orch.Read(ctx, r), nil
}

func (s *server) Write(
  ctx context.Context,
  r *writerp.WriteRequest,
) (*writerp.WriteResponse, error) {
  return s.orch.Write(ctx, r), nil
}
```

Now, for the `main()` function:

```go
// server/main.go

func main() {
  ctx, cancel := context.WithCancel(context.Background())

  lis, err := net.Listen("tcp", ":"+strconv.Itoa(shared.Port))
  if err != nil {
    log.Default().Fatalf("Failed to listen: %v", err)
  }

  grpcServer := grpc.NewServer(
    grpc.UnaryInterceptor(interceptors.NoOpAuthInterceptor),
    grpc.StreamInterceptor(interceptors.NoOpStreamAuthInterceptor),
```

```
)

orch := orchestrator.NewOrchestrator(ctx, shared.DbFile)
orch.Start()
s := newServer(orch)

readerp.RegisterReaderServer(grpcServer, s)
writerp.RegisterWriterServer(grpcServer, s)
reflection.Register(grpcServer)

slog.Info("Server is running on port " +
  strconv.Itoa(shared.Port) + "...")

// ... (0)

if err := grpcServer.Serve(lis); err != nil {
  log.Default().Fatalf("Failed to serve: %v", err)
}

// ... (1)
}
```

Note that we also pull the `DbFile` and the `Port` into shared constants:

```
// shared/constants.go

const (
  DbFile     = "/tmp/bd.db"
  Port       = 50000
  // ...
)
```

So far, `server` is straightforward and mostly boilerplate, but there's a problem: this server will run until it receives a termination signal, which will halt the database immediately, even if there are in-flight requests. Because of choices that we'll make further in the book, this will not pose a risk to correctness – such as a partial write – but it will cause issues like abrupt client connection failures. We should handle this gracefully instead by trapping the `Interrupt`, `SIGINT`, and `SIGTERM`signals and taking deliberate cancellation steps:

```
// server/main.go

// ... (0)

sigChan := make(chan os.Signal, 1)
signal.Notify(
  sigChan,
  os.Interrupt, syscall.SIGINT, syscall.SIGTERM)
var wg sync.WaitGroup
wg.Add(1)
```

```
go func() {
  defer wg.Done()
  select {
  case <-ctx.Done():
    return
  case sig := <-sigChan:
    slog.Info("Received signal. Shutting down.",
      "sig", sig.String())
    grpcServer.GracefulStop()
    cancel()
  }
}()

// ... (1)

wg.Wait()
slog.Info("Clean shutdown. Goodbye!")
```

Now, let's take a look at interceptors, which are like middleware for gRPC, allowing us to manipulate requests. This is often used for things like authentication, and in fact, our sample interceptor, `NoOpAuthInterceptor` (and its `Stream` analog), are placeholders for a real authentication mechanism.

```
// server/interceptors/auth.go

func NoOpAuthInterceptor(
  ctx context.Context,
  req interface{},
  info *grpc.UnaryServerInfo,
  handler grpc.UnaryHandler,
) (interface{}, error) {
  slog.Info("No-op auth interceptor",
    "method", info.FullMethod)
  return handler(ctx, req)
}

func NoOpStreamAuthInterceptor(
  srv interface{},
  ss grpc.ServerStream,
  info *grpc.StreamServerInfo,
  handler grpc.StreamHandler,
) error {
  slog.Info("No-op stream auth interceptor",
    "method", info.FullMethod)
  return handler(srv, ss)
}
```

While these allow all requests to pass unchecked, we could add arbitrary logic to verify that requests are permitted.

Chapter 5: Orchestrator

```go
// server/api/orchestrator.go

type Orchestrator interface {
  ReadLsqt(
    context.Context,
    *readerp.ReadLsqtRequest,
  ) *readerp.ReadLsqtResponse
  Read(
    context.Context,
    *readerp.ReadRequest,
  ) *readerp.ReadResponse
  Write(
    context.Context,
    *writerp.WriteRequest,
  ) *writerp.WriteResponse
}
```

Let's turn now to the `Orchestrator`, which will take requests from the `server` frontend and do four things:

- Verify that the request is sane
- Split the request into multiple operations for execution
- Execute the operations in the correct order
- Build a response to be sent to the user

From the outside, there are only three things that the orchestrator can do: read the `Lsqt`, read object (user) data, and write object data.

On the inside, there are three components that the orchestrator must use:

Component	Description
WAL	The write-ahead log, or `WAL`, will record all write operations prior to executing them. That way, if anything fails after we begin but before we finish writing data, we will be able to roll back or roll forward to a valid state.
AttrStore	The attribute store, or `AttrStore`, will store all of the raw field data. In our earlier telephone book example, this data might include fields like `firstName` and `streetAddress` along with the previously mentioned indexed fields.
IndexStore	The `IndexStore` will store all of the indexed properties such as `lastName`, `telephoneNumber`, and `recordId` from our telephone book example in a way that allows us to read them quickly.

Without saying anything about the implementations of those three components, let's start filling in the `Orchestrator`.

Heartbeats

The first thing that we should notice is that since a bitemporal database is always moving forward in transaction time, we need to keep our database moving forward. Before reviewing the implementation, let's consider what a user would observe during a period of no writes if we didn't manually tick the transaction time forward every so often:

Time	User action	Observed Lsqt after action
T0	Write	T0
T1	Write	T1
T2	Read	T1
T3	Read	T1
T4	Read	T1

Time	User action	Observed Lsqt after action
T5	Write	T5

Fixing this is easy to do with a heartbeat every second, an interval that we choose arbitrarily but that works well in practice. After implementing this, the user would see a timeline more akin to this, where "N+" indicates a value larger than N:

Time	User action	Observed Lsqt after action
T0	Write	T0
T1	Write	T1
T2	Read	T1+
T3	Read	T2+
T4	Read	T3+
T5	Write	T5

One complication is that we cannot blindly advance the `Tt` every second; we can only enqueue a new `Tt` to be advanced. This is because there may be ongoing writes with earlier assigned `Tt`s that haven't yet committed. Therefore, when a write begins, we add its assigned `Tt` to the set of `inFlightTts` and remove it once the write has completed normally. If there exists an `inFlightTt` that is earlier than a heartbeat `Tt`, then we cannot advance to that heartbeat `Tt` until the `inFlightTt` is removed from the set. We keep all heartbeat `Tt`s in the `pendingTts` heap until they can be advanced.

```
// server/orchestrator/orchestrator.go

// This must be called under pendingTtsLock.
func (o *Orchestrator) flushPendingTts() {
  o.inFlightTtsLock.Lock()
  for o.pendingTts.Len() > 0 {
    p := heap.Pop(o.pendingTts).(shared.Tt)
    if _, exists := o.inFlightTts[p]; exists {
      heap.Push(o.pendingTts, p)
      break
    }
    lsqt := shared.Lsqt(int64(p))
    err := o.walStore.WriteAdvanceLsqt(o.ctx, lsqt)
    if err != nil {
      log.Default().Fatal(
        "Failed to WriteAdvanceLsqt()",
        "err",
        err)
    }
    o.lsqtLock.Lock()
    o.lsqt = lsqt
    o.lsqtLock.Unlock()
```

```go
        slog.Info("Orchestrator", "lsqt", o.lsqt)
    }
    o.inFlightTtsLock.Unlock()
}

// server/orchestrator/orchestrator.go

func (o *Orchestrator) startHeartbeat() {
    tckr := time.NewTicker(1000 * time.Millisecond)
    go func() {
        for {
            select {
            case <-o.ctx.Done():
                return
            case <-tckr.C:
                tck := o.cl.tick()
                slog.Info("Orchestrator heartbeat", "tck", tck)
                o.pendingTtsLock.Lock()
                heap.Push(o.pendingTts, shared.Tt(tck))
                o.flushPendingTts()
                o.pendingTtsLock.Unlock()
            }
        }
    }()
}
```

At this point, we should be able to see the Lsqt ticking in a test by using a helper, getOrch, that sets up a test Orchestrator for us:

```go
// server/orchestrator/orchestrator_test.go

func TestHeartbeats(t *testing.T) {
    _ /*ctx*/, cancel, dbfile, o := getOrch(t)
    defer cancel()
    defer os.Remove(dbfile)
    lsqt0 := o.lsqt
    assert.Eventually(t, func() bool {
        o.lsqtLock.Lock()
        defer o.lsqtLock.Unlock()
        lsqt1 := o.lsqt
        return lsqt1.After(lsqt0)
    }, time.Second*5, time.Millisecond*500)
}
```

From the above code, it's clear that o.cl.tick() provides a new Tt, but we haven't yet said how it does so. While there's no explicit requirement that we use a wall clock, doing so simplifies queries because there's no need to map an arbitrary Tt to a time in the real world. Here's a simple implementation of a clock:

```go
// server/orchestrator/clock.go
```

```
type clock struct {
  lastTime int64
  lock     sync.Mutex
}

func newClock(lastTime shared.Tt) *clock {
  return &clock{
    lastTime: int64(lastTime),
  }
}

func (cl *clock) tick() shared.Tt {
  cl.lock.Lock()
  defer cl.lock.Unlock()
  t := time.Now().UnixMicro()
  if t <= cl.lastTime {
    cl.lastTime += 1
  } else {
    cl.lastTime = t
  }
  return shared.Tt(cl.lastTime)
}
```

To avoid time going backward – think of changing the system time! – the clock maintains the lastTime that it issued. If the system clock ever goes backward, the clocksimply advances its own lastTime. This solves the problem of a system time change while the database is running, but what if the time changes while the database is shut down? The clock may try to assign a past Tt, and doing so would rewrite history, which is prohibited. Therefore, on startup, we set lastTime to the last Tt written in the WAL. If there is no such Tt, like when we start the database for the first time, we'll use Tt = -1.

Reads

Now that time is moving forward on its own, let's implement reads. Although it is possible to implement queries that span time ranges, our database will require that every read takes place at the temporal coordinates that the user provides because this is the most common query type in this model. As an additional feature, it is possible to implement other types of reads, such as timelines, in which one temporal coordinate is fixed, and all versions of an object are loaded: "show me how ObjectId changed over time where tt = X," for example.

Before reading, the client must fetch the Lsqtso that it knows how far into the future it can read. Since the Orchestrator keeps the Lsqt in memory, this is trivial:

```
// server/orchestrator/orchestrator.go

func (o *Orchestrator) getLsqt() shared.Lsqt {
  o.lsqtLock.Lock()
  curLsqt := o.lsqt
  o.lsqtLock.Unlock()
  return curLsqt
}

func (o *Orchestrator) ReadLsqt(
  ctx context.Context,
  rr *readerp.ReadLsqtRequest,
) *readerp.ReadLsqtResponse {
  curLsqt := o.getLsqt()
  return &readerp.ReadLsqtResponse{
    ResponseType: readerp.ReadResponseType_SUCCESS,
    Lsqt:          int64(curLsqt),
  }
}
```

Now that we can serve the `Lsqt`, it's time to focus on reading objects. First, we have to verify that the request itself is sane – that it contains the correct fields, for example. If the request is not sane, then we'll return the BAD_REQUEST error type. Then, for reading by index(es), we have to verify that the given `Tt` is not after the current `Lsqt` since reading after the `Lsqt` would be akin to reading the future. If a read is beyond the `Lsqt`, then we'll return the FUTURE_TT error type. Next, whether to read by index(es) or to read a previous version of an object, we will read from the `IndexStore` and load the corresponding `Attrs` from the `AttrStore`. Finally, we'll return the response. If there's an error along the way, then we'll return INTERNAL. If there's no error, then we'll return UNKNOWN_ERROR, which is the default value for `ReadResponseErrorType`. (Don't worry—we'll define these errors in `reader.proto` in Chapter 9.) All three error types are listed below:

ReadResponseErrorType	Description
INTERNAL	Something unexpected happened internally, such as not being able to read data from disk.
BAD_REQUEST	The request failed precondition checks and is not sane.
FUTURE_TT	The request is for a `Tt` in the future.

Since reads don't modify any data, we don't need to write them to the WAL.

Let's validate that the read is sane:

```
// server/orchestrator/orchestrator.go

func (o *Orchestrator) validateRead(
```

```
    rr *readerp.ReadRequest,
) error {
  switch rr.RequestType {
  case readerp.ReadRequest_READ_INDEX_CONDITIONS:
    if rr.Tt <= 0 || rr.Vt <= 0 {
      return fmt.Errorf(
        "Invalid TemporalCoordinates (%+v, %+v)",
        rr.Tt,
        rr.Vt)
    } else if rr.TsId != "" {
      return fmt.Errorf("Unexpectedly received TsId")
    }
    break
  case readerp.ReadRequest_READ_PREVIOUS:
    if rr.Tt != 0 || rr.Vt != 0 {
      return fmt.Errorf(
        "Unexpectedly received TemporalCoordinates")
    } else if len(rr.TsId) == 0 {
      return fmt.Errorf(
        "Invalid TsId %+v",
        rr.TsId)
    }
    break
  default:
    return fmt.Errorf(
      "Unrecognized ReadRequestType %+v",
      rr.RequestType)
  }
  return nil
}
```

To fetch the `AttrIds` for an indexed read, we will go to the `IndexStore`:

```
// server/orchestrator/orchestrator.go

func (o *Orchestrator) processReadIndexConditions(
  ctx context.Context,
  rr *readerp.ReadRequest,
  curLsqt shared.Lsqt,
) (
  []*api.AttrIdMeta,
  *shared.TemporalCoordinates,
  readerp.ReadResponseErrorType,
) {
  tc := shared.NewTemporalCoordinates(
    shared.Tt(rr.Tt),
    shared.Vt(rr.Vt))
  if tc.Tt.AfterLsqt(curLsqt) {
    slog.Error(
      "tc.Tt.AfterLsqt()",
      "tc.Tt", tc.Tt,
```

```
      "curLsqt", curLsqt)
    return nil, nil, readerp.ReadResponseErrorType_FUTURE_TT
  }
  attrIdMetas, err := o.indexStore.Read(
    ctx,
    rr.IndexConditions,
    tc)
  if err != nil {
    slog.Error("indexStore.Read()", "err", err)
    return nil, nil, readerp.ReadResponseErrorType_INTERNAL
  }
  return attrIdMetas,
    tc,
    readerp.ReadResponseErrorType_UNKNOWN_ERROR
}
```

We will also go to the `IndexStore` to read the previous version of an object:

```
// server/orchestrator/orchestrator.go

func (o *Orchestrator) processReadPrevious(
  ctx context.Context,
  rr *readerp.ReadRequest,
) (
  []*api.AttrIdMeta,
  *shared.TemporalCoordinates,
  readerp.ReadResponseErrorType,
) {
  a, err := o.indexStore.ReadPreviousAttrId(
    ctx,
    shared.TsId(rr.TsId))
  if err != nil {
    slog.Error("indexStore.ReadPreviousAttrId()", "err", err)
    return nil, nil, readerp.ReadResponseErrorType_INTERNAL
  }
  return []*api.AttrIdMeta{a},
    shared.NewTemporalCoordinates(a.TtFrom, a.VtFrom),
    readerp.ReadResponseErrorType_UNKNOWN_ERROR
}
```

Once we have the `AttrIdMetas`, we can build `ReadObjects`, which are the objects to return to the client:

```
// server/orchestrator/orchestrator.go

func (o *Orchestrator) buildReadObjects(
  ctx context.Context,
  attrIdMetas []*api.AttrIdMeta,
  tc *shared.TemporalCoordinates,
  curLsqt shared.Lsqt,
) ([]*readerp.ReadResponse_ReadObject, error) {
```

```go
  attrIds := make([]shared.AttrId, len(attrIdMetas))
  objectIds := make([]shared.ObjectId, len(attrIdMetas))
  for idx, aoid := range attrIdMetas {
    attrIds[idx] = aoid.AttrId
    objectIds[idx] = shared.ObjectId(aoid.ObjectId)
  }
  lastWrites, err := o.indexStore.LastWrites(
    ctx, curLsqt, objectIds)
  if err != nil {
    return nil, err
  }
  attrsM, err := o.attrStore.Read(ctx, attrIds)
  if err != nil {
    return nil, err
  }
  readObjects := make(
    []*readerp.ReadResponse_ReadObject, 0, len(attrIdMetas))
  for idx, aoid := range attrIdMetas {
    attrs, exists := attrsM[aoid.AttrId]
    if !exists {
      return nil, fmt.Errorf("Missing Attrs for %+v",
aoid.AttrId)
    }
    if !attrs.IsTombstone {
      oid := objectIds[idx]
      lw, exists := lastWrites[oid]
      if !exists {
        return nil, fmt.Errorf("Missing LastWrite for %+v",
oid)
      }
      readObjects = append(
        readObjects,
        newReadObject(
          oid, attrs.Fqn, aoid.TsId, attrs.Data, lw,
          aoid.TtFrom, aoid.VtFrom, tc.Tt, tc.Vt))
    }
  }
  return readObjects, nil
}
```

Finally, we'll put it all together in `Read()`:

```go
// server/orchestrator/orchestrator.go

func (o *Orchestrator) Read(
  ctx context.Context,
  rr *readerp.ReadRequest,
) *readerp.ReadResponse {
  if err := o.validateRead(rr); err != nil {
    slog.Error("validateRead()", "err", err)
    return &readerp.ReadResponse{
```

```
      ResponseType:        readerp.ReadResponseType_FAIL,
      ResponseErrorType:
readerp.ReadResponseErrorType_BAD_REQUEST,
    }
  }
  var attrIdMetas []*api.AttrIdMeta
  var tc *shared.TemporalCoordinates
  var errType readerp.ReadResponseErrorType
  curLsqt := o.getLsqt()
  if rr.RequestType ==
readerp.ReadRequest_READ_INDEX_CONDITIONS {
    attrIdMetas, tc, errType =
      o.processReadIndexConditions(ctx, rr, curLsqt)
  } else if rr.RequestType == readerp.ReadRequest_READ_PREVIOUS
{
    attrIdMetas, tc, errType = o.processReadPrevious(ctx, rr)
  }
  if errType != readerp.ReadResponseErrorType_UNKNOWN_ERROR {
    return &readerp.ReadResponse{
      ResponseType:        readerp.ReadResponseType_FAIL,
      ResponseErrorType: errType,
    }
  }
  readObjects, err := o.buildReadObjects(
    ctx, attrIdMetas, tc, curLsqt)
  if err != nil {
    return &readerp.ReadResponse{
      ResponseType:        readerp.ReadResponseType_FAIL,
      ResponseErrorType:
readerp.ReadResponseErrorType_INTERNAL,
    }
  }
  return &readerp.ReadResponse{
    ResponseType: readerp.ReadResponseType_SUCCESS,
    ReadObjects:  readObjects,
  }
}
```

Note the `IsTombstone` field in `ReadObject`. We may read by `ObjectId` where the object has been deleted, so we'll read a tombstone entry that we'll implement in Chapter 7. `IsTombstone: true` corresponds to a tombstone, which means that the data was valid at a prior Tt and the Vt of the current read, but it was later deleted.

Using some no-op ("no operation") implementations of `AttrStore` and `IndexStore`, we can write some tests to verify the behavior of `Read()`.

```
// server/orchestrator/orchestrator_test.go

func TestReadAtFutureTt(t *testing.T) {
  ctx, cancel, dbfile, o := getOrch(t)
```

```
    defer cancel()
    defer os.Remove(dbfile)
    resp := o.Read(ctx, &readerp.ReadRequest{
      RequestType: readerp.ReadRequest_READ_INDEX_CONDITIONS,
      Tt:          math.MaxInt64,
      Vt:          int64(17),
    })
    assert.Equal(t,
      readerp.ReadResponseType_FAIL,
      resp.ResponseType)
    assert.Equal(t,
      readerp.ReadResponseErrorType_FUTURE_TT,
      resp.ResponseErrorType)
    assert.Empty(t, resp.ReadObjects)
}

// server/orchestrator/orchestrator_test.go

func TestReadAtValidTemporalCoordinates(t *testing.T) {
    ctx, cancel, dbfile, o := getOrch(t)
    defer cancel()
    defer os.Remove(dbfile)
    resp := o.Read(ctx, &readerp.ReadRequest{
      RequestType: readerp.ReadRequest_READ_INDEX_CONDITIONS,
      Tt:          int64(16),
      Vt:          int64(17),
    })
    assert.Equal(t,
      readerp.ReadResponseType_SUCCESS,
      resp.ResponseType)
    assert.Equal(t,
      readerp.ReadResponseErrorType_UNKNOWN_ERROR,
      resp.ResponseErrorType)
    assert.Empty(t, resp.ReadObjects)
}
```

Writes

Writes differ from reads in a crucial way: the database sets the Tt, not the user.
Let's consider why this must be so by imagining that the user can set the Tt on each
of the following writes:

Time	Tt assigned	Data written
T100	T150	a=1
T200	T175	a=2

If a user reads the value of a at $T180$, what should the result be? If we consider only
the first write, then a=1. However, the second write changes the value of a at a

previous time even though `a` has already been read. In other words, if we wait long enough after the first read at `T180`, then we may get a different result (`a=2`), a violation of referential transparency. This is the fundamental reason that the database is wholly responsible for assigning the `Tt` to each write.

Before assigning the `Tt`, the database must check that the request is sane. In addition to checking that the request is well-formed, there are several other errors that we must guard against. All eight error types are listed below:

`WriteResponseErrorType`	Description
INTERNAL	Something unexpected happened internally, such as not being able to write data to disk.
CONFLICT	The request includes a write to an `ObjectId` for which there is already an in-flight (or in-progress) write.
STALE	The `LastRead` for at least one of the given `ObjectIds` is before the `lastWrite` of that object.
BAD_REQUEST	The request failed precondition checks and is not sane.
UNFULL	At least one of the given `ObjectIds` references another `ObjectId` that does not exist at or before the `Lsqt`, and this request will not create it.
KEY_CONSTRAINT	At least one of the given `ObjectIds` has a key, but a write for that key is already in-flight.
IMPERMANENT_KEY	At least one of the given `ObjectIds` has a key whose value is different from the existing value of that key.
UNIQUE_CONSTRAINT	At least one of the given `ObjectIds` has a unique index whose value already exists at the given `TemporalCoordinates`, and this request will not resolve the conflict.

After assigning the `Tt`, the database must write the data to the WAL. This guarantees that if any part of the write fails before it finishes – if someone unplugs the machine, for example – then the data can be recovered. (We will return to recovery in Chapter 6.) Once data is durable in the WAL, the user's data is written to the `AttrStore`. Finally, the metadata can be written to the `IndexStore`. Only then can we commit the transaction by flushing the assigned `Tt`. The act of flushing the `Tt` allows the database to advance the `Lsqt` to that point, making writes that took place at or before that `Tt` permanently visible to readers.

As with reads, we will begin by validating that the write request is sane:

```
// server/orchestrator/orchestrator.go

func (o *Orchestrator) validateWriteRequest(
  wr *writerp.WriteRequest,
) error {
  switch wr.RequestType {
  case writerp.WriteRequest_PUT:
    for _, wo := range wr.WriteObjects {
      if err := o.validatePut(wo); err != nil {
        return err
      }
    }
    break
  case writerp.WriteRequest_DELETE:
    for _, wo := range wr.WriteObjects {
      if err := o.validateDelete(wo); err != nil {
        return err
      }
    }
    break
  case writerp.WriteRequest_RESTORE:
    for _, wo := range wr.WriteObjects {
      if err := o.validateRestore(wo); err != nil {
        return err
      }
    }
    break
  default:
    return fmt.Errorf(
      "Unrecognized WriteRequestType %+v",
      wr.RequestType)
  }
  return nil
}
```

We will use different logic to validate each of PUT, DELETE, and RESTORE:

```
// server/orchestrator/orchestrator.go

func (o *Orchestrator) validatePut(
  wo *writerp.WriteRequest_WriteObject,
) error {
  err := o.validateWriteObject(wo)
  if err != nil {
    return err
  }
  if len(wo.Attrs) == 0 {
    return fmt.Errorf("Empty Attrs")
  } else if len(wo.TsId) > 0 {
    return fmt.Errorf("Non-empty TsId")
  }
```

```
    return nil
}

// server/orchestrator/orchestrator.go

func (o *Orchestrator) validateDelete(
  wo *writerp.WriteRequest_WriteObject,
) error {
  err := o.validateWriteObject(wo)
  if err != nil {
    return err
  }
  if len(wo.Attrs) != 0 {
    return fmt.Errorf("Non-empty Attrs")
  } else if len(wo.TsId) > 0 {
    return fmt.Errorf("Non-empty TsId")
  }
  return nil
}

// server/orchestrator/orchestrator.go

func (o *Orchestrator) validateRestore(
  wo *writerp.WriteRequest_WriteObject,
) error {
  err := o.validateWriteObject(wo)
  if err != nil {
    return err
  }
  if len(wo.TsId) == 0 {
    return fmt.Errorf("Empty TsId")
  }
  return nil
}
```

We also need to check that no in-flight write conflicts with this one. How might they conflict? Suppose that there was an in-flight write to some `ObjectId` when we begin the current write, and this request also writes the same `ObjectId`. Since the writes would be in-flight at the same time and they cannot finish simultaneously, one of them must finish first. Since the second one to finish began before the first one finished, it cannot possibly know the correct `lastWrite`. Therefore, we can reject it immediately. The same holds for writes to key and unique index properties, although we'll check them in a later function.

```
// server/orchestrator/orchestrator.go

func (o *Orchestrator) checkInFlightWrites(
  wr *writerp.WriteRequest,
) error {
  o.inFlightObjectIdsLock.Lock()
```

```go
  for _, wo := range wr.WriteObjects {
    if _, exists :=
      o.inFlightObjectIds[shared.ObjectId(wo.ObjectId)]; exists
{
      o.inFlightObjectIdsLock.Unlock()
      return fmt.Errorf(
        "In-flight write conflict: %s", wo.ObjectId)
    }
  }
  for _, wo := range wr.WriteObjects {
    o.inFlightObjectIds[shared.ObjectId(wo.ObjectId)] =
struct{}{}
  }
  o.inFlightObjectIdsLock.Unlock()
  return nil
}
```

Speaking of `lastWrite`, we must verify that the given objects have the correct values for `lastWrite`:

```go
// server/orchestrator/orchestrator.go

func (o *Orchestrator) verifyLastWrites(
  ctx context.Context,
  wr *writerp.WriteRequest,
  curLsqt shared.Lsqt,
  requiredObjectIds []shared.ObjectId,
) (map[shared.ObjectId]shared.Tt,
writerp.WriteResponseErrorType) {
  lastWrites, err := o.indexStore.LastWrites(
    ctx, curLsqt, requiredObjectIds)
  if err != nil {
    slog.Error("Write()", "err", err)
    return nil, writerp.WriteResponseErrorType_INTERNAL
  }
  for _, wo := range wr.WriteObjects {
    oid := shared.ObjectId(wo.ObjectId)
    if lastWrites[oid].After(shared.Tt(wo.LastRead)) {
      slog.Error("Write()",
        "oid", oid,
        "lastWrites[oid]", lastWrites[oid],
        "wo.LastRead", wo.LastRead)
      return nil, writerp.WriteResponseErrorType_STALE
    }
  }
  return lastWrites,
writerp.WriteResponseErrorType_UNKNOWN_ERROR
}
```

For simplicity, let's group those checks:

```
// server/orchestrator/orchestrator.go

func (o *Orchestrator) verifyPreEnrich(
  ctx context.Context,
  wr *writerp.WriteRequest,
) writerp.WriteResponseErrorType {
  // Verify that we can process this write type.
  if err := o.validateWriteRequest(wr); err != nil {
    slog.Error("verifyPreEnrich()", "wr", wr, "err",
err.Error())
    return writerp.WriteResponseErrorType_BAD_REQUEST
  }
  // Verify that there is no in-flight write for this ObjectId.
  if err := o.checkInFlightWrites(wr); err != nil {
    slog.Error("verifyPreEnrich()", "wr", wr, "err",
err.Error())
    return writerp.WriteResponseErrorType_CONFLICT
  }
  // Verify that all refs exist.
  haveObjectIds, mustVerifyAlreadyExistObjectIds :=
    o.getObjectIdsToVerify(wr)
  // Verify that lastWrite is at least as large as LastWrite().
  requiredObjectIds := append(
    haveObjectIds,
    mustVerifyAlreadyExistObjectIds...)
  lastWrites, errType := o.verifyLastWrites(
    ctx,
    wr,
    o.getLsqt(),
    requiredObjectIds)
  if errType != writerp.WriteResponseErrorType_UNKNOWN_ERROR {
    return errType
  }
  // Verify that referenced ObjectIds already exist.
  for _, oid := range mustVerifyAlreadyExistObjectIds {
    if !lastWrites[oid].After(shared.Tt(-1)) {
      slog.Error(
        "verifyPreEnrich()",
        "oid", oid,
        "lastWrites[oid]", lastWrites[oid])
      return writerp.WriteResponseErrorType_UNFULL
    }
  }
  return writerp.WriteResponseErrorType_UNKNOWN_ERROR
}
```

By default, we index by `ObjectId` and by `Fqn`, so let's add those index values:

```
// server/orchestrator/orchestrator.go

func (o *Orchestrator) enrichIndexConditions(
```

```
    wr *writerp.WriteRequest,
) {
  for _, wo := range wr.WriteObjects {
    wo.IndexConditions = append(
      wo.IndexConditions,
      &indexp.IndexCondition{
        Key:             shared.ObjectIdKey,
        Op:              indexp.IndexConditionOp_EQUAL,
        IsObjectIdValue: true,
        Value: &indexp.IndexCondition_ObjectIdValue{
          ObjectIdValue: wo.ObjectId,
        },
      })
    // Always make this the last element in the list so that we
    // can reference it below.
    wo.IndexConditions = append(
      wo.IndexConditions,
      &indexp.IndexCondition{
        Key:         shared.FqnKey,
        Op:          indexp.IndexConditionOp_EQUAL,
        IsFqnValue: true,
        Value: &indexp.IndexCondition_FqnValue{
          FqnValue: wo.Fqn,
        },
      })
  }
}
```

Those checks have been mostly lock-free, allowing the server to process multiple requests in parallel. At this point, we must take some extra locks and check in-flight keys and unique indexes. The checks are nearly identical:

```
// server/orchestrator/orchestrator.go

func (o *Orchestrator) verifyInFlightKey(
  ctx context.Context,
  ic *indexp.IndexCondition,
  fqn shared.Fqn,
  oid shared.ObjectId,
) (uint64, writerp.WriteResponseErrorType) {
  if _, exists := o.inFlightKeys[fqn]; !exists {
    o.inFlightKeys[fqn] = make(
      map[string]map[uint64]struct{})
  }
  h := o.hashIndexCondition(ic)
  if vs, exists := o.inFlightKeys[fqn][ic.Key]; exists {
    if _, exists := vs[h]; exists {
      slog.Error(
        "KEY_CONSTRAINT check",
        "ic", ic,
        "h", h,
```

```
      "vs", vs)
      return 0, writerp.WriteResponseErrorType_KEY_CONSTRAINT
    }
  } else {
    o.inFlightKeys[fqn][ic.Key] = make(map[uint64]struct{})
  }
  o.inFlightKeys[fqn][ic.Key][h] = struct{}{}
  return h, writerp.WriteResponseErrorType_UNKNOWN_ERROR
}

// server/orchestrator/orchestrator.go

func (o *Orchestrator) verifyInFlightUIdx(
  ctx context.Context,
  ic *indexp.IndexCondition,
  fqn shared.Fqn,
  oid shared.ObjectId,
) (uint64, writerp.WriteResponseErrorType) {
  if _, exists := o.inFlightUIdxs[fqn]; !exists {
    o.inFlightUIdxs[fqn] = make(
      map[string]map[uint64]struct{})
  }
  h := o.hashIndexCondition(ic)
  if vs, exists :=
    o.inFlightUIdxs[fqn][ic.Key]; exists {
    if _, exists := vs[h]; exists {
      slog.Error(
        "UNIQUE_CONSTRAINT check",
        "ic", ic,
        "h", h,
        "vs", vs)
      return 0,
writerp.WriteResponseErrorType_UNIQUE_CONSTRAINT
    }
  } else {
    o.inFlightUIdxs[fqn][ic.Key] =
      make(map[uint64]struct{})
  }
  o.inFlightUIdxs[fqn][ic.Key][h] = struct{}{}
  return h, writerp.WriteResponseErrorType_UNKNOWN_ERROR
}
```

A simple loop over all `WriteObjects` completes this class of checks:

```
// server/orchestrator/orchestrator.go

func (o *Orchestrator) verifyInFlightKeysAndUIdxs(
  ctx context.Context,
  wr *writerp.WriteRequest,
) ([]*inFlightUniqueishIndex,
  []*inFlightUniqueishIndex,
```

33

```
    writerp.WriteResponseErrorType,
) {
  o.inFlightKeysLock.Lock()
  defer o.inFlightKeysLock.Unlock()
  o.inFlightUIdxsLock.Lock()
  defer o.inFlightUIdxsLock.Unlock()
  toRemoveInFlightKeys := make([]*inFlightUniqueishIndex, 0)
  toRemoveInFlightUIdxs := make([]*inFlightUniqueishIndex, 0)
  for _, wo := range wr.WriteObjects {
    fqn := shared.Fqn(wo.Fqn)
    oid := shared.ObjectId(wo.ObjectId)
    for _, ic := range wo.IndexConditions {
      if ic.IsKey {
        h, errType := o.verifyInFlightKey(ctx, ic, fqn, oid)
        if errType !=
          writerp.WriteResponseErrorType_UNKNOWN_ERROR {
          return toRemoveInFlightKeys, toRemoveInFlightUIdxs,
            errType
        }
        toRemoveInFlightKeys = append(toRemoveInFlightKeys,
          newInFlightUniqueishIndex(fqn, ic.Key, h))
      } else if ic.IsUnique {
        h, errType := o.verifyInFlightUIdx(
          ctx, ic, fqn, oid)
        if errType !=
          writerp.WriteResponseErrorType_UNKNOWN_ERROR {
          return toRemoveInFlightKeys, toRemoveInFlightUIdxs,
            errType
        }
        toRemoveInFlightUIdxs = append(toRemoveInFlightUIdxs,
          newInFlightUniqueishIndex(fqn, ic.Key, h))
      }
    }
  }
  return toRemoveInFlightKeys, toRemoveInFlightUIdxs,
    writerp.WriteResponseErrorType_UNKNOWN_ERROR
}
```

It's insufficient to check only in-flight keys and unique indexes, however; we must also check existing values. From this point onward, we'll need the Tt of the write, so let's assign it:

```
// server/orchestrator/orchestrator.go

func (o *Orchestrator) makeInFlightTt() shared.Tt {
  assignedTt := o.cl.tick()
  o.inFlightTtsLock.Lock()
  o.inFlightTts[assignedTt] = struct{}{}
  o.inFlightTtsLock.Unlock()
  o.pendingTtsLock.Lock()
  heap.Push(o.pendingTts, assignedTt)
```

```
    o.pendingTtsLock.Unlock()
    return assignedTt
}
```

Since `assignedTt` is now in-flight, the caller will `defer` the following function to flush it:

```
// server/orchestrator/orchestrator.go

func (o *Orchestrator) maybeFlushTt(tt shared.Tt) {
  o.inFlightTtsLock.Lock()
  delete(o.inFlightTts, tt)
  o.inFlightTtsLock.Unlock()
  o.pendingTtsLock.Lock()
  o.flushPendingTts()
  o.pendingTtsLock.Unlock()
}
```

Why is it called `maybeFlushTt()` instead of `flushTt()`? Even though `tt` will no longer be marked in-flight, other writes with earlier assigned `Tts` may still be in-flight. We cannot advance the `Lsqt` past an in-flight transaction, so we must always wait for the earliest in-flight `Tt` to flush. This suggests an interesting optimization opportunity: assign `Tts` based on the predicted duration of the write so that writes that are likely to be ready to flush earlier have smaller `Tts`, and writes that are likely to be ready to flush later have larger `Tts`. We will leave this as an exercise for the reader.

With the `assignedTt` we can check the existing keys and unique indexes to ensure that the write will not violate a constraint. This time, the checks are somewhat different because while keys are permanent, unique indexes may change over time.

```
// server/orchestrator/orchestrator.go

func (o *Orchestrator) verifyExistingKey(
  ctx context.Context,
  ic *indexp.IndexCondition,
  fqn shared.Fqn,
  oid shared.ObjectId,
) writerp.WriteResponseErrorType {
  // If there is an existing object with the given key at
  // any TemporalCoordinates, then the existing ObjectId
  // must match the incoming ObjectId. Otherwise, it's a
  // KEY_CONSTRAINT error.
  existingOid, err := o.indexStore.ReadKey(ctx, ic, fqn)
  if err != nil {
    slog.Error("verifyExistingKey()", "err", err)
    return writerp.WriteResponseErrorType_INTERNAL
  }
  if !existingOid.IsNil() && existingOid != oid {
```

```go
      return writerp.WriteResponseErrorType_KEY_CONSTRAINT
    }
    // If this ObjectId has already been written, then its key
    // must not change.
    ok, err := o.indexStore.VerifyKey(
      ctx, ic, oid, fqn)
    if err != nil || !ok {
      ret := writerp.WriteResponseErrorType_INTERNAL
      if err == nil {
        ret = writerp.WriteResponseErrorType_IMPERMANENT_KEY
      }
      return ret
    }
  }
  return writerp.WriteResponseErrorType_UNKNOWN_ERROR
}

// server/orchestrator/orchestrator.go

func (o *Orchestrator) verifyExistingUIdx(
  ctx context.Context,
  wr *writerp.WriteRequest,
  ic *indexp.IndexCondition,
  oidIc *indexp.IndexCondition,
  fqn shared.Fqn,
  oid shared.ObjectId,
  assignedTt shared.Tt,
  vtFrom shared.Vt,
) writerp.WriteResponseErrorType {
  // Incoming ObjectId matches existing ObjectId.
  icsToCheck := []*indexp.IndexCondition{ic, oidIc}
  attrIds, err := o.indexStore.Read(ctx, icsToCheck,
    shared.NewTemporalCoordinates(assignedTt, vtFrom))
  if err != nil {
    slog.Error("verifyExistingUIdx()", "err", err)
    return writerp.WriteResponseErrorType_INTERNAL
  }
  if len(attrIds) > 1 {
    return writerp.WriteResponseErrorType_INTERNAL
  } else if len(attrIds) == 1 &&
    oid != attrIds[0].ObjectId {
    // Swapping unique values among ObjectIds in this request.
    safeToProceed := false
    for _, wo2 := range wr.WriteObjects {
      if safeToProceed {
        break
      }
      if shared.ObjectId(wo2.ObjectId) == attrIds[0].ObjectId {
        for _, ic2 := range wo2.IndexConditions {
          if o.indexConditionSameKeyDifferentValues(ic, ic2) {
            safeToProceed = true
            break
```

```
        }
      }
    }
  }
  if !safeToProceed {
    return writerp.WriteResponseErrorType_UNIQUE_CONSTRAINT
  }
}
return writerp.WriteResponseErrorType_UNKNOWN_ERROR
}
```

As before, a simple loop over all `WriteObjects` will complete this class of checks:

```
// server/orchestrator/orchestrator.go

func (o *Orchestrator) verifyExistingKeysAndUIdxs(
  ctx context.Context,
  wr *writerp.WriteRequest,
  assignedTt shared.Tt,
) writerp.WriteResponseErrorType {
  if wr.RequestType != writerp.WriteRequest_PUT {
    return writerp.WriteResponseErrorType_UNKNOWN_ERROR
  }
  for _, wo := range wr.WriteObjects {
    for _, ic := range wo.IndexConditions {
      fqn := shared.Fqn(wo.Fqn)
      oid := shared.ObjectId(wo.ObjectId)
      if ic.IsKey {
        errType := o.verifyExistingKey(ctx, ic, fqn, oid)
        if errType !=
          writerp.WriteResponseErrorType_UNKNOWN_ERROR {
          return errType
        }
      } else if ic.IsUnique {
        errType := o.verifyExistingUIdx(
          ctx, wr,
          ic, wo.IndexConditions[len(wo.IndexConditions)-1],
          fqn, oid, assignedTt, shared.Vt(wo.VtFrom))
        if errType !=
          writerp.WriteResponseErrorType_UNKNOWN_ERROR {
          return errType
        }
      }
    }
  }
  return writerp.WriteResponseErrorType_UNKNOWN_ERROR
}
```

If this is a DELETE, verify that we're deleting an existing object. We cannot delete if the given `TemporalCoordinates` are in empty space:

```
// server/orchestrator/orchestrator.go

func (o *Orchestrator) verifySaneDelete(
  ctx context.Context,
  wr *writerp.WriteRequest,
  assignedTt shared.Tt,
) writerp.WriteResponseErrorType {
  if wr.RequestType != writerp.WriteRequest_DELETE {
    return writerp.WriteResponseErrorType_UNKNOWN_ERROR
  }
  for _, wo := range wr.WriteObjects {
    attrIdMetas, err := o.indexStore.Read(
      ctx, wo.IndexConditions, shared.NewTemporalCoordinates(
        assignedTt, shared.Vt(wo.VtFrom)))
    if err != nil {
      slog.Error("verifySaneDelete()", "err", err)
      return writerp.WriteResponseErrorType_INTERNAL
    }
    if len(attrIdMetas) == 0 {
      return writerp.WriteResponseErrorType_BAD_REQUEST
    }
    attrIds := make([]shared.AttrId, len(attrIdMetas))
    for idx, aoid := range attrIdMetas {
      attrIds[idx] = aoid.AttrId
    }
    attrsM, err := o.attrStore.Read(ctx, attrIds)
    if err != nil || len(attrsM) != len(attrIds) {
      if err != nil {
        slog.Error("verifySaneDelete()", "err", err)
      }
      return writerp.WriteResponseErrorType_INTERNAL
    }
    for _, a := range attrsM {
      if a.IsTombstone {
        return writerp.WriteResponseErrorType_BAD_REQUEST
      }
    }
  }
  return writerp.WriteResponseErrorType_UNKNOWN_ERROR
}
```

Having made it through so many validation steps, we can now write the Attrs. If this fails, we don't need to be too concerned because there will be no entries in the IndexStore that reference, or point to, these Attrs. Therefore, they will never be loaded. A useful optimization would be to remove them, likely asynchronously.

There are two cases. In the case of RESTORE, we know that we already have the Attrs written for the previous version, so all we have to do is look them up:

```
// server/orchestrator/orchestrator.go
```

```
func (o *Orchestrator) attrIdsForRestore(
  ctx context.Context,
  wr *writerp.WriteRequest,
) ([]*shared.Attrs, error) {
  allAttrs := make([]*shared.Attrs, len(wr.WriteObjects))
  allTsIds := make([]shared.TsId, len(wr.WriteObjects))
  for i, wo := range wr.WriteObjects {
    allTsIds[i] = shared.TsId(wo.TsId)
  }
  attrIdsM, err := o.indexStore.ReadAttrIds(ctx, allTsIds)
  if err != nil {
    slog.Error("attrIdsForRestore()", "err", err)
    return nil, err
  }
  for i, wo := range wr.WriteObjects {
    if attrId, exists := attrIdsM[shared.TsId(wo.TsId)]; exists
{
      allAttrs[i] = &shared.Attrs{
        AttrId: attrId,
      }
    } else {
      err := fmt.Errorf("Missing attrId with TsId %+v",
wo.TsId)
      return nil, err
    }
  }
  return allAttrs, nil
}
```

In all other cases – namely, PUT and DELETE – we write new Attrs:

```
// server/orchestrator/orchestrator.go

func (o *Orchestrator) writeAttrs(
  ctx context.Context,
  wr *writerp.WriteRequest,
) ([]*shared.Attrs, error) {
  allAttrs := make([]*shared.Attrs, len(wr.WriteObjects))
  for i, wo := range wr.WriteObjects {
    oid := shared.ObjectId(wo.ObjectId)
    fqn := shared.Fqn(wo.Fqn)
    aid := shared.NewAttrId()
    isDelete := wr.RequestType == writerp.WriteRequest_DELETE
    allAttrs[i] = shared.NewAttrs(
      aid,
      oid,
      fqn,
      wo.Attrs,
      isDelete)
  }
```

```
  err := o.attrStore.Write(ctx, allAttrs)
  if err != nil {
    slog.Error("writeAttrs()", "err", err)
    return nil, err
  }
  return allAttrs, nil
}
```

Now, to write the indexes:

```
// server/orchestrator/orchestrator.go

func (o *Orchestrator) writeIndexes(
  ctx context.Context,
  wr *writerp.WriteRequest,
  tx *sql.Tx,
  assignedTt shared.Tt,
  allAttrs []*shared.Attrs,
) error {
  for i, wo := range wr.WriteObjects {
    oid := shared.ObjectId(wo.ObjectId)
    fqn := shared.Fqn(wo.Fqn)
    tc := shared.NewTemporalCoordinates(
      assignedTt,
      shared.Vt(wo.VtFrom))
    var prevTsId shared.TsId
    if wr.RequestType == writerp.WriteRequest_RESTORE {
      prevTsId = shared.TsId(wo.TsId)
    }
    err := o.indexStore.Write(
      tx,
      api.NewIndexStoreWrite(oid, fqn, allAttrs[i].AttrId,
        shared.NewTsId(), prevTsId,
        wo.IndexConditions, tc))
    if err != nil {
      slog.Error("writeIndexes()", "err", err)
      return err
    }
  }
  return nil
}
```

We need to handle those transactionally with our backend, so let's wrap
`writeIndexes()` in a storage-level transaction. Note that this does constrain our
choice of backing store to one that supports ACID transactions. Fortunately,
choices abound.

```
// server/orchestrator/orchestrator.go

func (o *Orchestrator) writeAndCommitIndexes(
```

```
    ctx context.Context,
    wr *writerp.WriteRequest,
    assignedTt shared.Tt,
    allAttrs []*shared.Attrs,
) error {
    tx, err := o.db.Begin()
    if err != nil {
        return err
    }
    err = o.writeIndexes(ctx, wr, tx, assignedTt, allAttrs)
    if err != nil {
        slog.Error("writeAndCommitIndexes()", "err", err)
        err2 := tx.Rollback()
        if err2 != nil {
            // This has to be fatal because we don't know the state
of
            // the data on disk. It requires manual intervention.
            log.Default().Fatal("writeAndCommitIndexes()", "err2",
err2)
        }
        return err
    }
    return tx.Commit()
}
```

Since we wrapped the validations in a function, let's wrap the backend writing, too:

```
// server/orchestrator/orchestrator.go

func (o *Orchestrator) doWrite(
    ctx context.Context,
    wr *writerp.WriteRequest,
) (shared.Tt, writerp.WriteResponseErrorType) {
    // Assign the Tt.
    assignedTt := o.makeInFlightTt()
    defer o.maybeFlushTt(assignedTt)
    // Verify that key and unique index constraints are not
violated.
    errType := o.verifyExistingKeysAndUIdxs(ctx, wr, assignedTt)
    if errType != writerp.WriteResponseErrorType_UNKNOWN_ERROR {
        return assignedTt, errType
    }
    // If this is a delete, are we trying to delete in empty
space
    // or in an existing tombstone?
    errType = o.verifySaneDelete(ctx, wr, assignedTt)
    if errType != writerp.WriteResponseErrorType_UNKNOWN_ERROR {
        return assignedTt, errType
    }
    var allAttrs []*shared.Attrs
    var err error
```

```go
  if wr.RequestType == writerp.WriteRequest_RESTORE {
    // If this is a RESTORE, then avoid some writes by using
the
    // existing AttrId associated with the given TsId.
    allAttrs, err = o.attrIdsForRestore(ctx, wr)
  } else {
    // Otherwise, write the new Attrs.
    allAttrs, err = o.writeAttrs(ctx, wr)
  }
  err = o.writeAndCommitIndexes(ctx, wr, assignedTt, allAttrs)
  if err != nil {
    slog.Error("doWrite()", "err", err)
    return assignedTt, writerp.WriteResponseErrorType_INTERNAL
  }
  // Don't allow a successful write to finish until it can take
  // this lock.
  o.finishWriteLock.Lock()
  o.finishWriteLock.Unlock()
  return assignedTt,
writerp.WriteResponseErrorType_UNKNOWN_ERROR
}
```

Finally, we'll complete `Write()`. Notice that we `defer` removing items from the various in-flight lists so that once a request has completed and `Write()` has returned, subsequent requests can touch those same items.

```go
// server/orchestrator/orchestrator.go

func (o *Orchestrator) Write(
  ctx context.Context,
  wr *writerp.WriteRequest,
) *writerp.WriteResponse {
  errType := o.verifyPreEnrich(ctx, wr)
  defer o.removeInFlightObjectIds(wr)
  if errType != writerp.WriteResponseErrorType_UNKNOWN_ERROR {
    return &writerp.WriteResponse{
      ResponseType:      writerp.WriteResponseType_FAIL,
      ResponseErrorType: errType,
    }
  }
  // Enrich IndexConditions.
  o.enrichIndexConditions(wr)
  // Verify in-flight keys and unique indexes.
  toRemoveInFlightKeys, toRemoveInFlightUIdxs, errType :=
    o.verifyInFlightKeysAndUIdxs(ctx, wr)
  defer o.clearInFlightKeysAndUIdxs(
    toRemoveInFlightKeys,
    toRemoveInFlightUIdxs)
  if errType != writerp.WriteResponseErrorType_UNKNOWN_ERROR {
    return &writerp.WriteResponse{
```

```
      ResponseType:        writerp.WriteResponseType_FAIL,
      ResponseErrorType: errType,
    }
  }
  assignedTt, errType := o.doWrite(ctx, wr)
  if errType != writerp.WriteResponseErrorType_UNKNOWN_ERROR {
    return &writerp.WriteResponse{
      ResponseType:        writerp.WriteResponseType_FAIL,
      ResponseErrorType: errType,
    }
  }
  return &writerp.WriteResponse{
    ResponseType: writerp.WriteResponseType_SUCCESS,
    Tt:            int64(assignedTt),
  }
}
```

Having finished the implementation of reads and writes, let's turn to the WAL, the AttrStore, and the IndexStore.

Chapter 6: WAL

```go
// server/api/wal.go

type Wal interface {
  ReadLastTt(
    context.Context,
  ) (shared.Tt, error)
  ReadSinceLastAdvanceLsqt(
    context.Context,
  ) ([]*walp.WalEntry, error)
  WriteAdvanceLsqt(
    context.Context,
    shared.Lsqt,
  ) error
  WriteUserWrite(
    context.Context,
    shared.Lsqt,
    *writerp.WriteRequest,
  ) error
}
```

Before we change any data in the database, we'll write the operation to the WAL, or Write-Ahead Log. This way, if any operation is interrupted or otherwise fails, we can roll backward or forward as appropriate to get the database back into a valid state. How far back must we roll back? We can be certain that a write has completed only after an `AdvanceLsqt` with a larger `Tt` is written to the WAL. Therefore, on startup, the database must first check the most recent WAL entry. If the most recent entry is not `AdvanceLsqt`, then we must roll back until the most recent such entry.

Let's look at two cases.

Time	Event
T0	Write0
T1	Write1
T2	AdvanceLsqt
T3	Power goes out

Once the power is restored, what must we do to restore the database? Since we wrote `AdvanceLsqt` at `T2` and performed no additional writes, we know that all prior writes – those at `T0` and `T1` – finished completely. Since `AdvanceLsqt` is idempotent, we can re-run that WAL entry to ensure that the `Lsqt` is set correctly, then resume normal operation, including heartbeats and user queries.

Time	Event
T0	Write0
T1	AdvanceLsqt
T2	Write1
T3	Write2
T4	Power goes out

In this case, we don't know whether or not the writes at `T2` and `T3` completed. Therefore, once the power is restored, we must either roll forward or roll back both `Write2` and `Write1`. Only then can we resume normal operation.

Because it's a bit tricky to roll back writes to a bitemporal space, we're going to choose to roll forward and wrap each bitemporal space write in a transaction within our backend. Of course, rolling back writes to the `AttrStore` is easy because all rows are independent of one another, so we could freely delete ones that we want to roll back. However, it doesn't matter if we leave some unused ones stored on the rare case of unclean shutdown—since no bitemporal rectangle has that `attr_id`, the data will never be loaded. For these reasons, we can omit a rollback step entirely. We can instead know that operations that can be read, like writes to the `IndexStore`, are complete. All we need to do is to apply each WAL entry written after the most recent `AdvanceLsqt` in an idempotent way. (Remember: just because an operation was written to the WAL doesn't mean that it was written to the `AttrStore` or to the `IndexStore`.) Then, we must ensure that the first `Tt` that the database ticks is at least as large as the largest `Tt` in our WAL.

Our WAL will be stored in a SQLite table with the following structure:

WAL
tt INTEGER NOT NULL
kind TEXT NOT NULL
data BLOB NOT NULL

Since we will support only `AdvanceLsqt` and `WriteRequest` WAL entries, we'll use a `CHECK CONSTRAINT` on kind: `CHECK(kind IN ('A','W'))`.

With an index on `tt`, we will be able to quickly find the most recent WAL entries on startup. But what will those entries look like? Let's define them as protos:

```
// proto/server/wal/wal.proto

message AdvanceLsqt {
  int64 lsqt = 1;
}

message WalEntry {
  enum WalEntryType {
    UNKNOWN = 0;
    ADVANCE_LSQT = 1;
    WRITE_REQUEST = 2;
  }

  WalEntryType type = 1;
  oneof value {
    AdvanceLsqt advance_lsqt = 2;
    writer.WriteRequest write_request = 3;
  }
}
```

Now, let's first implement a generic "write this proto to the WAL" method:

```
// server/wal/wal.go

func (w *Wal) insert(
  lsqt shared.Lsqt,
  kind string,
  we *walp.WalEntry,
) error {
```

```go
  anyProto, err := anypb.New(we)
  if err != nil {
    return err
  }
  anyProtoBytes, err := proto.Marshal(anyProto)
  if err != nil {
    return err
  }
  _, err = w.db.Exec(`
    INSERT INTO wal VALUES(?,?,?);
  `, int64(lsqt), kind, anyProtoBytes)
  return err
}
```

Now, let's implement writing `AdvanceLsqt`:

```go
// server/wal/wal.go

func (w *Wal) WriteAdvanceLsqt(
  ctx context.Context,
  lsqt shared.Lsqt,
) error {
  al := &walp.AdvanceLsqt{
    Lsqt: int64(lsqt),
  }
  we := &walp.WalEntry{
    Type: walp.WalEntry_ADVANCE_LSQT,
    Value: &walp.WalEntry_AdvanceLsqt{
      AdvanceLsqt: al,
    },
  }
  return w.insert(lsqt, advanceLsqtKind, we)
}
```

User writes – that is, write requests from users – are persisted similarly:

```go
// server/wal/wal.go

func (w *Wal) WriteUserWrite(
  ctx context.Context,
  lsqt shared.Lsqt,
  wr *writerp.WriteRequest,
) error {
  we := &walp.WalEntry{
    Type: walp.WalEntry_WRITE_REQUEST,
    Value: &walp.WalEntry_WriteRequest{
      WriteRequest: wr,
    },
  }
  return w.insert(lsqt, writeRequestKind, we)
}
```

Since we need to get the most recent `Tt` on startup, let's implement that:

```
// server/wal/wal.go

func (w *Wal) ReadLastTt(
  ctx context.Context,
) (shared.Tt, error) {
  var tt shared.Tt
  if err := w.db.QueryRow(`
    SELECT tt FROM wal ORDER BY tt DESC LIMIT 1
  `).Scan(&tt); err != nil {
    if err == sql.ErrNoRows {
      return shared.Tt(-1), nil
    }
    return shared.Tt(-1), err
  }
  return tt, nil
}
```

Lastly, we need to get the operations to roll forward on startup. To make it easier to collect that data, we'll use a private `struct`:

```
// server/wal/wal.go

type walRow struct {
  tt    int64
  kind string
  data []byte
}
```

And with that, we can read the operations:

```
// server/wal/wal.go

func (w *Wal) ReadSinceLastAdvanceLsqt(
  ctx context.Context,
) ([]*walp.WalEntry, error) {
  rows, err := w.db.Query(`
    WITH x AS (
      SELECT tt FROM wal WHERE kind = ?
      ORDER BY tt DESC LIMIT 1
    )
    SELECT wal.* FROM wal, x WHERE wal.tt >= x.tt
  `, advanceLsqtKind)
  if err != nil {
    return nil, err
  }
  defer rows.Close()
  walEntries := make([]*walp.WalEntry, 0)
  for rows.Next() {
```

```go
  wr := &walRow{}
  err = rows.Scan(&wr.tt, &wr.kind, &wr.data)
  if err != nil {
    return nil, err
  }
  msgProto := &anypb.Any{}
  err = proto.Unmarshal(wr.data, msgProto)
  if err != nil {
    return nil, err
  }
  m, err := msgProto.UnmarshalNew()
  if err != nil {
    return nil, err
  }
  we, ok := m.(*walp.WalEntry)
  if !ok {
    return nil, fmt.Errorf(
      "Failed to convert %+v to *walp.WalEntry", m)
  }
  walEntries = append(walEntries, we)
}
return walEntries, nil
}
```

Chapter 7: AttrStore

```go
// server/api/attr_store.go

type AttrStore interface {
  Read(
    context.Context,
    []shared.AttrId,
  ) (map[shared.AttrId]*shared.Attrs, error)
  Write(
    context.Context,
    []*shared.Attrs,
  ) error
}
```

The `AttrStore` ("Attribute Store") will store the user's data, which corresponds to the fields of their models. This is how we might represent the telephone book example from earlier:

```
type Person struct {
  RecordId     int `bd:"key"`
  FirstName    string
  LastName     string `bd:"index"`
  PhoneNumber  string `bd:"unique"`
}

var myPerson = &Person{
  RecordId:     1,
  FirstName:    "Alice",
  LastName:     "Bronson",
  PhoneNumber: "555-1212",
}
```

We can (and will!) represent `myPerson` as JSON:

```
{"RecordId":1,
 "FirstName":"Alice",
 "LastName":"Bronson",
 "PhoneNumber":"555-1212"}
```

Of course, that omits type information. How will our database know to create an instance of `Person` from that JSON document? The answer is simple: it won't! Type metadata will be stored in the database, but it is the client that will hydrate objects of some type (like `Person`) using the JSON documents returned by the database. We will get to the client in Chapter 9. For now, let's focus on the `AttrStore`'s responsibility, which is to act as a key/value store of `AttrId` → `Attrs`.

In addition to the `id` (`AttrId`) and the properties (`data`), we need the `ObjectId`, the `Fqn`, and `IsTombstone`:

ATTRS
id TEXT NOT NULL
object_id TEXT NOT NULL
fqn TEXT NOT NULL
data BLOB NOT NULL
is_tombstone BOOLEAN NOT NULL

`is_tombstone` tells us that we wrote a DELETE here, so although there's no `data` here, the entry has meaning. (You may have seen this strategy elsewhere, such as in a hash table that uses open addressing.) To enforce that `data` and `is_tombstone` are mutually exclusive – that is, that each set of attributes either has data or is marked as a tombstone – we include a CONSTRAINT:

```
CHECK (
  (data IS NOT NULL AND NOT is_tombstone)
  OR
  (data IS NULL AND is_tombstone)
)
```

Because all of the reads will be by id, we'll include an index on that column.

The most interesting aspect of how we implement Read() is how we avoid SQL injection. We generate a slice of placeholders, each of which is a question mark, exactly as long as the slice of AttrIds. We put this slice of placeholders directly into our SQL query, and we rely on the database/sql library to sanitize the slice of args that will replace them. In all other respects, this is a simple multikey lookup:

```
// server/attrstore/attr_store.go

func (a *AttrStore) Read(
  ctx context.Context,
  aids []shared.AttrId,
) (map[shared.AttrId]*shared.Attrs, error) {
  placeholders := slices.Repeat([]string{"?"}, len(aids))
  args := make([]interface{}, len(aids))
  for i, aid := range aids {
    args[i] = aid
  }
  rows, err := a.db.Query(fmt.Sprintf(`
    SELECT id, object_id, fqn, data, is_tombstone
    FROM attrs
    WHERE id IN (%s)
  `, strings.Join(placeholders, ",")), args...)
  if err != nil {
    return nil, err
  }
  m := make(map[shared.AttrId]*shared.Attrs)
  defer rows.Close()
  for rows.Next() {
    var aid shared.AttrId
    var oid shared.ObjectId
    var fqn shared.Fqn
    var data []byte
    var isTombstone bool
    err = rows.Scan(&aid, &oid, &fqn, &data, &isTombstone)
    if err != nil {
      return nil, err
    }
    m[aid] = shared.NewAttrs(aid, oid, fqn, data, isTombstone)
  }
```

```
  return m, nil
}
```

Writes use the same trick to generate the correct number of placeholders and to sanitize the `args`:

```
// server/attrstore/attr_store.go

func (a *AttrStore) Write(
  ctx context.Context,
  attrs []*shared.Attrs,
) error {
  placeholders := slices.Repeat(
    []string{"(?,?,?,?,?)"}, len(attrs))
  args := make([]interface{}, len(attrs)*5)
  i := 0
  for _, attr := range attrs {
    args[i]   = attr.AttrId
    args[i+1] = attr.ObjectId
    args[i+2] = attr.Fqn
    args[i+3] = attr.Data
    args[i+4] = attr.IsTombstone
    i += 5
  }
  _, err := a.db.Exec(fmt.Sprintf(`
    INSERT INTO attrs VALUES %s;
  `, strings.Join(placeholders, ",")), args...)
  return err
}
```

Chapter 8: IndexStore

```go
// server/api/index_store.go

type IndexStore interface {
  LastWrites(
    context.Context,
    shared.Lsqt,
    []shared.ObjectId,
  ) (map[shared.ObjectId]shared.Tt, error)
  Read(
    context.Context,
    []*indexp.IndexCondition,
    *shared.TemporalCoordinates,
  ) ([]*AttrIdMeta, error)
  ReadAttrIds(
    context.Context,
    []shared.TsId,
  ) (map[shared.TsId]shared.AttrId, error)
  ReadPreviousAttrId(
    context.Context,
    shared.TsId,
  ) (*AttrIdMeta, error)
  ReadKey(
    context.Context,
    *indexp.IndexCondition,
    shared.Fqn,
  ) (shared.ObjectId, error)
  VerifyKey(
    context.Context,
    *indexp.IndexCondition,
    shared.ObjectId,
    shared.Fqn,
  ) (bool, error)
  Write(
    *sql.Tx,
    *IndexStoreWrite,
  ) error
}
```

The `IndexStore` is responsible for maintaining the bitemporal spaces. In order to support fast lookups, each indexed attribute of each object in the database will have its own row:

INDEXSTORE
tt_from INTEGER NOT NULL
tt_to INTEGER NOT NULL
vt_from INTEGER NOT NULL
vt_to INTEGER NOT NULL
object_id TEXT NOT NULL
fqn TEXT NOT NULL
field_name TEXT NOT NULL
field_value_int INTEGER
field_value_real REAL
field_value_string TEXT
attr_id TEXT NOT NULL

Notice that the temporal coordinates appear in every row. This is because the bitemporal space is composed of rectangles that each reference some data (some `Attrs`, in our database). The first time an object is written, it will be written with a never-before-seen `object_id`. Its `tt_from` and `vt_from` will be set by the database and by the user, respectively, and the `tt_to` and `vt_to` will be infinite, which we'll denote with `math.MaxInt64`. When we execute a read query, we will use the given `TemporalCoordinates` to filter the set of rows to consider.

You may be wondering why a new rectangle cannot have finite bounds. The answer is simple: we cannot predict the future. We cannot know when the database will record some new state of the data, and we cannot know what the valid time will be when (or if) that happens, so we cannot know what finite bounds to apply. At the time of the write, our knowledge is that the data has not yet changed.

When there is a new write to an existing bitemporal space, we have to be careful to avoid creating overlapping rectangles since an area of overlap would indicate that two versions of data were valid at the same time. But how could that be? It simply can't be the case that two versions are valid simultaneously.

There are six cases to consider when writing a new version, W, at the (tt, vt) denoted by *:

Case 1

We are writing the first data to a new bitemporal space for this `ObjectId`.

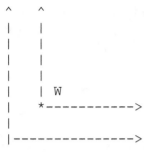

Case 2

We are writing a new version to an existing bitemporal space for this `ObjectId`. The `tt` is greater than the existing version's `ttFrom`, but the `vt` is less than the existing version's `vtFrom`.

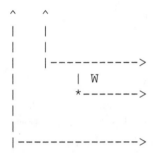

Case 3

We are writing a new version to an existing bitemporal space for this `ObjectId`. Both the `tt` and the `vt` are greater than the `ttFrom` and `vtFrom` of the existing version.

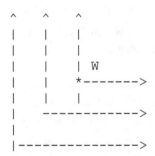

Case 4

We are writing a new version to an existing bitemporal space for this `ObjectId`. The `tt` is greater than the `ttFrom` of the existing version, and the `vt` is equal to the `vtFrom` of the existing version.

```
^       ^       ^
```

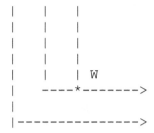

Case 5

We are writing a new version to an existing bitemporal space for this `ObjectId`. The `tt` is greater than the `ttFrom` of the existing version, the `vt` is equal to the `vtFrom` of the existing version, and there is an another timeslice at the same `tt` with a larger `vtFrom`.

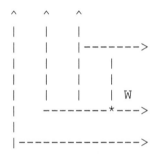

Case 6

We are writing a new version to an existing bitemporal space for this `ObjectId`. Both the `tt` and the `vt` are greater than the `ttFrom` and `vtFrom` of the existing version, and there is an another timeslice at the same `tt` with a larger `vtFrom`.

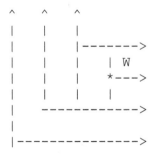

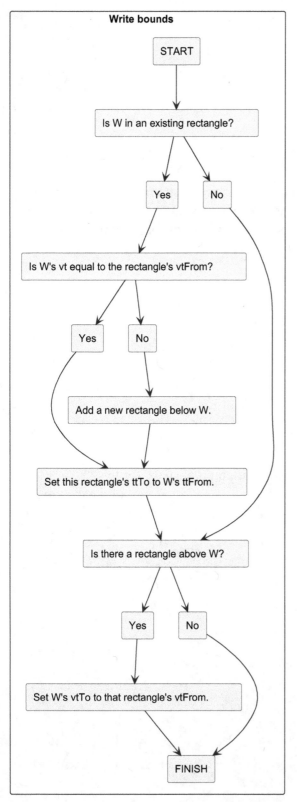

The flowchart to the left describes what operations to perform and what temporal bounds to choose for a write W based on the initial conditions of the bitemporal space. Unless otherwise specified, `ttTo` and `vtTo` are set to infinity (`math.MaxInt64`) when a rectangle is created.

Let's start by implementing `LastWrites()` since it's rather straightforward. All we have to do is look up the `tt_from` of the most recently written rectangle for each given `ObjectId`:

```go
// server/indexstore/index_store.go

func (i *IndexStore) LastWrites(
  ctx context.Context,
  lsqt shared.Lsqt,
  oids []shared.ObjectId,
) (map[shared.ObjectId]shared.Tt, error) {
  placeholders := slices.Repeat([]string{"?"}, len(oids))
  args := make([]interface{}, len(oids)+1)
  for i, oid := range oids {
    args[i] = oid
  }
  args[len(oids)] = int64(lsqt)
  rows, err := i.db.Query(fmt.Sprintf(`
    WITH t AS (
      SELECT object_id, tt_from, ROW_NUMBER() OVER (
        PARTITION BY object_id ORDER BY tt_from DESC
      ) AS rank
      FROM indexes
      WHERE object_id IN (%s)
        AND tt_from <= ?
    )
    SELECT object_id, tt_from FROM t WHERE rank = 1
  `, strings.Join(placeholders, ",")), args...)
  if err != nil {
    return nil, err
  }
  m := make(map[shared.ObjectId]shared.Tt)
  defer rows.Close()
  for rows.Next() {
    var oid shared.ObjectId
    var ttFrom shared.Tt
    if err = rows.Scan(&oid, &ttFrom); err != nil {
      return nil, err
    }
    m[oid] = ttFrom
  }
  for _, oid := range oids {
    if _, exists := m[oid]; !exists {
      m[oid] = shared.Tt(-1)
    }
  }
  return m, nil
}
```

The most interesting part of that function is the use of the window function PARTITION BY that allows us to fetch the maximum tt_from within groups (ObjectIds) rather than the maximum for all of them.

ReadKey() is also a very simple function; it returns the ObjectId that matches the given key, if it exists. If this key is already taken by a different ObjectId, it will lead to a KEY_CONSTRAINT error in the Orchestrator. Note the buildQ() function that constructs the SQL query; it uses the same placeholder trick that we saw in the AttrStore, and luckily, that function can be reused in several more places.

```go
// server/indexstore/index_store.go

func (i *IndexStore) buildQ(
  ic *indexp.IndexCondition,
  tc *shared.TemporalCoordinates,
  fqn shared.Fqn,
) (string, []interface{}, error) {
  var fieldValueFieldName string
  args := make([]interface{}, 0)
  placeholder := "?"
  if ic.Op == indexp.IndexConditionOp_IN {
    fieldValueFieldName = "field_value_string"
    placeholder = "(" + strings.Join(
      slices.Repeat([]string{"?"}, len(ic.ObjectIds)),
      ",") + ")"
    for _, oid := range ic.ObjectIds {
      args = append(args, oid)
    }
  } else {
    f, a := i.getFieldNameAndValue(ic)
    fieldValueFieldName = f
    args = append(args, a)
  }
  q := `SELECT attr_id, object_id, ts_id, tt_from, vt_from
        FROM indexes
        WHERE ` + fieldValueFieldName + ` ` +
    i.indexOpToString(ic.Op) + ` ` + placeholder
  if tc != nil {
    q += `AND tt_from <= ?
          AND tt_to > ?
          AND vt_from <= ?
          AND vt_to > ?
          AND field_name = ?`
    args = append(args, []interface{}{
      tc.Tt, tc.Tt, tc.Vt, tc.Vt, ic.Key}...)
  } else if !fqn.IsNil() {
    q += " AND fqn = ?"
    args = append(args, fqn)
```

```
  } else {
    return "", nil, fmt.Errorf("Expected tc or non-nil Fqn")
  }
  return q, args, nil
}
```

And `ReadKey()` itself:

```
// server/indexstore/index_store.go

func (i *IndexStore) ReadKey(
  ctx context.Context,
  ic *indexp.IndexCondition,
  fqn shared.Fqn,
) (shared.ObjectId, error) {
  q, args, err := i.buildQ(ic, nil, fqn)
  if err != nil {
    slog.Error("ReadKey()", "err", err)
    return shared.ObjectId(""), err
  }
  rows, err := i.db.Query(q, args...)
  if err != nil {
    slog.Error("ReadKey()", "err", err)
    return shared.ObjectId(""), err
  }
  defer rows.Close()
  for rows.Next() {
    var attrId shared.AttrId
    var oid shared.ObjectId
    var tsId shared.TsId
    var ttFrom shared.Tt
    var vtFrom shared.Vt
    err = rows.Scan(&attrId, &oid, &tsId, &ttFrom, &vtFrom)
    if err != nil {
      slog.Error("ReadKey()", "err", err)
      return shared.ObjectId(""), err
    }
    return shared.ObjectId(oidS), nil
  }
  return shared.ObjectId(""), nil
}
```

`VerifyKey()` is very similar: it checks that if this `ObjectId` already exists, then its key is not changing in this request. If its key is changing, then it will cause an `IMPERMANENT_KEY` error in the `Orchestrator`.

```
// server/indexstore/index_store.go

func (i *IndexStore) VerifyKey(
  ctx context.Context,
```

```
    ic *indexp.IndexCondition,
    oid shared.ObjectId,
    fqn shared.Fqn,
) (bool, error) {
    fieldName, fieldValue := i.getFieldNameAndValue(ic)
    q := fmt.Sprintf(`
      SELECT 1
      FROM indexes
      WHERE object_id = ?
        AND fqn = ?
        AND field_name = ?
        AND %s != ?
      LIMIT 1`, fieldName)
    args := []interface{}{oid, fqn, ic.Key, fieldValue}
    var x int
    err := i.db.QueryRow(q, args...).Scan(&x)
    if err == sql.ErrNoRows {
      return true, nil
    } else if err != nil {
      slog.Error("verifyKey()", "err", err.Error())
      return false, err
    }
    return false, nil
}
```

Now, we must implement `Read()`, which will read metadata for the objects that match the user query. It's important that we return metadata only for those entries that match *all* of the indexes, so after collecting all entries, we do some filtering:

```
// server/indexstore/index_store.go

func (i *IndexStore) filterAttrIds(
  icsCount int,
  attrIdsCounts map[shared.AttrId]int,
  attrIdsToMeta map[shared.AttrId]*api.AttrIdMeta,
) ([]*api.AttrIdMeta, error) {
  filteredAidsM := make(map[shared.AttrId]struct{})
  for aid, c := range attrIdsCounts {
    if c == icsCount {
      filteredAidsM[aid] = struct{}{}
    }
  }
  filteredAids := make([]shared.AttrId, len(filteredAidsM))
  idx := 0
  for aid := range filteredAidsM {
    filteredAids[idx] = aid
    idx += 1
  }
  res := make([]*api.AttrIdMeta, len(filteredAids))
  for idx, aid := range filteredAids {
    if aidMeta, exists := attrIdsToMeta[aid]; exists {
```

```
      res[idx] = aidMeta
    } else {
      return nil,
        fmt.Errorf("Cannot find AttrIdMeta for AttrId %+v",
aid)
    }
  }
  return res, nil
}
```

And Read() itself:

```
// server/indexstore/index_store.go
func (i *IndexStore) Read(
  ctx context.Context,
  ics []*indexp.IndexCondition,
  tc *shared.TemporalCoordinates,
) ([]*api.AttrIdMeta, error) {
  attrIdsCounts := make(map[shared.AttrId]int)
  attrIdsWithMeta := make(map[shared.AttrId]*api.AttrIdMeta)
  icsCount := 0
  for _, idx := range ics {
    if idx.Op == indexp.IndexConditionOp_IN &&
      len(idx.ObjectIds) == 0 {
      continue
    }
    icsCount += 1
    q, args, err := i.buildQ(idx, tc, shared.Fqn(""))
    if err != nil {
      return nil, err
    }
    rows, err := i.db.Query(q, args...)
    if err != nil {
      return nil, err
    }
    defer rows.Close()
    for rows.Next() {
      var aid shared.AttrId
      var oid shared.ObjectId
      var tsId shared.TsId
      var ttFrom shared.Tt
      var vtFrom shared.Vt
      err = rows.Scan(&aid, &oid, &tsId, &ttFrom, &vtFrom)
      if err != nil {
        return nil, err
      }
      if _, exists := attrIdsCounts[aid]; !exists {
        attrIdsCounts[aid] = 0
        attrIdsWithMeta[aid] = api.NewAttrIdMeta(
          aid, oid, tsId, ttFrom, vtFrom)
```

```
      }
      attrIdsCounts[aid] += 1
    }
  }
  return i.filterAttrIds(icsCount, attrIdsCounts,
attrIdsWithMeta)
}
```

To implement `Write()`, we'll use a `struct`, `rectangleRow`, and a small function, `insertRow()`, to insert new index rows:

```
// server/indexstore/index_store.go

type rectangleRow struct {
  tsId       shared.TsId
  prevTsId   shared.TsId
  ttFrom     shared.Tt
  ttTo       shared.Tt
  vtFrom     shared.Vt
  vtTo       shared.Vt
  objectId   shared.ObjectId
  fqn        shared.Fqn
  fieldName  string
  attrId     shared.AttrId
}
```

```
// server/indexstore/index_store.go

func (i *IndexStore) insertRow(
  tx *sql.Tx,
  idx *indexp.IndexCondition,
  row *rectangleRow,
) error {
  args := make([]interface{}, 11)
  args[0] = row.tsId
  if !row.prevTsId.IsNil() {
    args[1] = row.prevTsId
  }
  args[2] = row.ttFrom
  args[3] = row.ttTo
  args[4] = row.vtFrom
  args[5] = row.vtTo
  args[6] = row.objectId
  args[7] = row.fqn
  args[8] = row.fieldName
  args[10] = row.attrId
  fieldValueKind := "field_value_string"
  if idx.Op != indexp.IndexConditionOp_IN {
    fieldValueKind, args[9] = i.getFieldNameAndValue(idx)
  }
  q := `INSERT INTO indexes (
```

```
            ts_id, prev_ts_id,
            tt_from, tt_to,
            vt_from, vt_to,
            object_id, fqn,
            field_name, ` + fieldValueKind + `,
            attr_id) VALUES (?,?,?,?,?,?,?,?,?,?,?)`
  if idx.Op == indexp.IndexConditionOp_IN {
    // This is the refs case. Other cases have single values.
    for _, oid := range idx.ObjectIds {
      args[9] = oid
      _, err := tx.Exec(q, args...)
      if err != nil {
        return err
      }
    }
    return nil
  }
  _, err := tx.Exec(q, args...)
  return err
}
```

If the write is within an existing timeslice, then we have to close it before writing the new one:

```
// server/indexstore/index_store.go

func (i *IndexStore) closeExistingTimeslice(
  tx *sql.Tx,
  oid shared.ObjectId,
  fqn shared.Fqn,
  ics []*indexp.IndexCondition,
  tc *shared.TemporalCoordinates,
  existsTtFrom shared.Tt,
  existsVtFrom shared.Vt,
  existsAid shared.AttrId,
) error {
  _, err := tx.Exec(`
    UPDATE indexes SET tt_to = ?
    WHERE object_id = ? AND tt_from = ? AND vt_from = ?
  `, tc.Tt, oid, existsTtFrom, existsVtFrom)
  if err != nil {
    slog.Error("closeExistingTimeslice()", "err", err)
    return err
  }
  // If W's vt > the existing vtFrom, then we have to insert a
  // rectangle under W.
  if tc.Vt.After(existsVtFrom) {
    for _, idx := range ics {
      err = i.insertRow(tx, idx, newRectangleRow(
        shared.NewTsId(), shared.TsId(""),
        tc.Tt, shared.Tt(math.MaxInt64), existsVtFrom, tc.Vt,
```

```
        oid, fqn, idx.Key, existsAid))
      if err != nil {
        slog.Error("closeExistingTimeslice()", "err", err)
        return err
      }
    }
  }
  return nil
}
```

We also need to check whether or not it really is in an existing timeslice:

```
// server/indexstore/index_store.go

func (i *IndexStore) closeExistingTimesliceIfExists(
  tx *sql.Tx,
  oid shared.ObjectId,
  fqn shared.Fqn,
  ics []*indexp.IndexCondition,
  tc *shared.TemporalCoordinates,
) (shared.Vt, shared.Vt, error) {
  var existsTtFrom shared.Tt
  var existsVtFrom, existsVtTo shared.Vt
  var existsAid shared.AttrId
  var err error
  row := i.db.QueryRow(`
    SELECT tt_from, vt_from, vt_to, attr_id FROM indexes
    WHERE object_id = ?
      AND tt_from <= ? AND tt_to > ?
      AND vt_from <= ? AND vt_to > ?
    LIMIT 1
  `, oid, tc.Tt, tc.Tt, tc.Vt, tc.Vt)
  exists := true
  if err = row.Scan(
    &existsTtFrom, &existsVtFrom,
    &existsVtTo, &existsAid); err == sql.ErrNoRows {
    exists = false
  } else if err != nil {
    slog.Error("closeExistingTimesliceIfExists()", "err", err)
    return shared.Vt(0), shared.Vt(0), err
  }
  if exists {
    err = i.closeExistingTimeslice(
      tx, oid, fqn, ics, tc,
      existsTtFrom, existsVtFrom, existsAid)
    if err != nil {
      slog.Error("closeExistingTimesliceIfExists()", "err",
err)
      return shared.Vt(0), shared.Vt(0), err
    }
  }
```

```
  return existsVtFrom, existsVtTo, nil
}
```

Once we have closed the existing timeslice, if it exists, we need to insert the new one:

```
// server/indexstore/index_store.go

func (i *IndexStore) insertTimeslice(
  tx *sql.Tx,
  oid shared.ObjectId,
  fqn shared.Fqn,
  aid shared.AttrId,
  tsId shared.TsId,
  prevTsId shared.TsId,
  ics []*indexp.IndexCondition,
  tc *shared.TemporalCoordinates,
  existsVtFrom shared.Vt,
  existsVtTo shared.Vt,
) error {
  vtTo := shared.Vt(math.MaxInt64)
  if existsVtTo > 0 {
    vtTo = existsVtTo
  } else {
    // If W is not in an existing rectangle, then check above.
    row := i.db.QueryRow(`
      SELECT vt_from FROM indexes
      WHERE object_id = ?
        AND tt_from <= ? AND tt_to > ? AND vt_from > ?
      ORDER BY vt_from LIMIT 1
    `, oid, tc.Tt, tc.Tt, tc.Vt)
    if err := row.Scan(&existsVtFrom); err != nil &&
      err != sql.ErrNoRows {
      slog.Error("insertTimeslice()", "err", err)
      return err
    } else if err == nil {
      vtTo = existsVtFrom
    }
  }
  for _, idx := range ics {
    err := i.insertRow(tx, idx, newRectangleRow(tsId, prevTsId,
      tc.Tt, shared.Tt(math.MaxInt64), tc.Vt, vtTo,
      oid, fqn, idx.Key, aid))
    if err != nil {
      slog.Error("insertTimeslice()", "err", err)
      return err
    }
  }
  return nil
}
```

Finally, we can implement `Write()`:

```go
// server/indexstore/index_store.go

func (i *IndexStore) Write(
  tx *sql.Tx,
  isWrite *api.IndexStoreWrite,
) error {
  if len(ics) == 0 {
    return nil
  }
  existsVtFrom, existsVtTo, err :=
    i.closeExistingTimesliceIfExists(
      tx, isWrite.ObjectId, isWrite.Fqn, isWrite.Ics,
isWrite.Tc)
  if err != nil {
    return err
  }
  return i.insertTimeslice(
    tx, isWrite.ObjectId, isWrite.Fqn, isWrite.AttrId,
    isWrite.TsId, isWrite.PrevTsId,
    isWrite.Ics, isWrite.Tc,
    existsVtFrom, existsVtTo)
}
```

To save some work in the `Orchestrator`, we read and reuse `AttrIds` on `RESTORE`. Let's see what `ReadAttrIds()` looks like:

```go
// server/indexstore/index_store.go

func (i *IndexStore) ReadAttrIds(
  ctx context.Context,
  tsIds []shared.TsId,
) (map[shared.TsId]shared.AttrId, error) {
  if len(tsIds) == 0 {
    return nil, nil
  }
  placeholder := strings.Join(
    slices.Repeat([]string{"?"}, len(tsIds)), ",")
  args := make([]interface{}, len(tsIds))
  for i, tsId := range tsIds {
    args[i] = tsId
  }
  q := `SELECT ts_id, attr_id FROM indexes
    WHERE ts_id IN (` + placeholder + `) GROUP BY ts_id`
  rows, err := i.db.Query(q, args...)
  if err != nil {
    slog.Error("ReadAttrIds()", "err", err)
    return nil, err
  }
```

```go
  defer rows.Close()
  m := make(map[shared.TsId]shared.AttrId)
  for rows.Next() {
    var tsId shared.TsId
    var attrId shared.AttrId
    err = rows.Scan(&tsId, &attrId)
    if err != nil {
      slog.Error("ReadAttrIds()", "err", err)
      return nil, err
    }
    m[tsId] = attrId
  }
  return m, nil
}
```

When we want to read the previous version of an object, we'll use
ReadPreviousAttrId():

```go
// server/indexstore/index_store.go

func (i *IndexStore) ReadPreviousAttrId(
  ctx context.Context,
  tsId shared.TsId,
) (*api.AttrIdMeta, error) {
  row := i.db.QueryRow(`
    SELECT pre.attr_id, pre.object_id, pre.ts_id,
      pre.tt_from, pre.vt_from
    FROM indexes i
    JOIN indexes pre
      ON i.prev_ts_id = pre.ts_id
    WHERE i.ts_id = ?
    LIMIT 1`, tsId)
  var attrId shared.AttrId
  var objectId shared.ObjectId
  var tsIdTmp shared.TsId
  var ttFrom shared.Tt
  var vtFrom shared.Vt
  var err error
  exists := true
  if err = row.Scan(&attrId, &objectId, &tsIdTmp,
    &ttFrom, &vtFrom); err == sql.ErrNoRows {
    exists = false
  } else if err != nil {
    slog.Error("ReadPreviousAttrId()", "err", err)
    return nil, err
  }
  if exists {
    return &api.AttrIdMeta{
      AttrId:   attrId,
      ObjectId: objectId,
      TsId:     tsIdTmp,
```

```
        TtFrom:    ttFrom,
        VtFrom:    vtFrom,
    }, nil
  }
  return nil, fmt.Errorf("Not found")
}
```

Chapter 9: Client

```go
// client/api/client.go

type Client interface {
  CatchUp(
    shared.Tt, int,
  ) (shared.Tt, error)
  GetLsqt() (shared.Tt, error)
  Get(
    *cshared.IndexedQuery,
    *shared.TemporalCoordinates,
  ) (*cshared.BdObjectIterator, error)
  GetRef(
    *cshared.RefMeta,
  ) (cshared.BdObjectI, error)
  GetRefs(
    *cshared.RefMeta,
  ) (*cshared.BdObjectIterator, error)
  Put(
    cshared.BdObjectI,
    shared.Vt,
  ) (shared.Tt, error)
  MultiPut(
    []cshared.BdObjectI,
    shared.Vt,
  ) (shared.Tt, error)
  Delete(
    cshared.BdObjectI,
    shared.Vt,
  ) (shared.Tt, error)
  MultiDelete(
    []cshared.BdObjectI,
    shared.Vt,
  ) (shared.Tt, error)
}
```

Now that we have a working database, we need a client; otherwise, we'll have to manually write gRPC commands to communicate with it. For our client, we'll assume that users already have some classes that they would like to read and write, and we'll generate code to make that easy. Fortunately, this is a cinch with Go. But first, let's look at some behavior that we would like our `Client` to have by imagining that we have some existing models:

```
type Certification struct {
  cshared.BdObject
  Name string `bd:"unique"`
}

type Department struct {
  cshared.BdObject
  Name string `bd:"unique"`
}

type Employee struct {
  cshared.BdObject
  Id              int `bd:"key"`
  FirstName       string
  LastName        string            `bd:"index"`
  TenureRank      int               `bd:"unique"`
  _department     *Department       `bd:"ref"`
  _certifications []*Certification  `bd:"refs"`
}
```

There are a lot of things to review here. First, notice that `cshared.BdObject` (short for "client shared bitemporal database object") is embedded inside `Employee`. `cshared.BdObject` is a base `struct` that provides common fields and functions, such as the temporal coordinates at which the object was read.

Note also the use of Go tags such as `"index"` and `"unique"`. We will use these to generate extra behaviors:

Tag	Description
index	This field may be used for fast indexed lookups, such as looking up an `Employee` by their `LastName`. More than one object may have the same value at a given (tt, vt).
unique	Only one object at a given (tt, vt) may have this value, such as the name of a `Certification` or of a `Department`. This field may be used for fast indexed lookups.
key	Only one object may ever have this value, and once set, the value cannot be changed. This may be something like a unique `Id` assigned by an employer and can be used for fast indexed lookups.

Tag	Description
ref	This field refers to another cshared.BdObject, such as how an Employee belongs to exactly one Department.
refs	This field refers to a (possibly empty) list of other cshared.BdObjects, such as how an Employee may have zero or more Certifications.

Since FirstName has no tags, it will be persisted but will not be available for querying.

But what even is a BdObject? It's simply a class that implements the interface BdObjectI:

```go
// client/shared/bd_object_i.go

type BdObjectI interface {
  ObjectId() gshared.ObjectId
  SetObjectId(gshared.ObjectId)
  Fqn() gshared.Fqn
  SetFqn(gshared.Fqn)
  Data() []byte
  IsTombstone() bool
  LastRead() gshared.Tt
  TtFrom() gshared.Tt
  VtFrom() gshared.Vt
  TtResolvedAt() gshared.Tt
  VtResolvedAt() gshared.Vt
  IndexConditions() []*indexp.IndexCondition
  ToJson() ([]byte, error)
  TsId() gshared.TsId
  SetTsId(gshared.TsId)
}
```

And the BdObject class itself:

```go
// client/shared/bd_object.go

var _ BdObjectI = &BdObject{}

type BdObject struct {
  objectId      gshared.ObjectId
  fqn           gshared.Fqn
  data          []byte
  isTombstone   bool
  lastRead      gshared.Tt
  ttFrom        gshared.Tt
  vtFrom        gshared.Vt
  ttResolvedAt  gshared.Tt
  vtResolvedAt  gshared.Vt
  tsId          gshared.TsId
```

```
}
```

The accessors for each of these properties are elided since they're trivial.

Meanwhile, back to `Certification`, `Department`, and `Employee`...here's how we might use those objects.

```
operations := NewDepartment("Operations")
cfa := NewCertification("CFA")
mba := NewCertification("MBA")
e := NewEmployee(
  1, "Alice", "Andrews", 7, operations,
  []*Certification{cfa, mba},
)
vt := shared.VtOf(
  time.Date(2010, time.June, 25, 0, 0, 0, 0, time.UTC))
// Save Alice, Operations, CFA, and MBA.
tt, _ /*err*/ := cli.MultiPut(
  []cshared.BdObjectI{
    e, operations, cfa, mba,
  }, vt)
// Make sure we're caught up.
tt, _ /*err*/ = cli.CatchUp(tt, 5000)
// Find all people with the last name "Andrews."
es, _ /*err*/ := cli.Get(
  NewEmployeeQuery().LastNameEq("Andrews").Build(),
  shared.NewTemporalCoordinates(tt, vt))
for _, e := range NewEmployeeIterator(es).Items() {
  slog.Info("Employee",
    "FirstName", e.FirstName, "LastName", e.LastName)
}
// Find the five people with the longest tenure and their
// Certifications and Departments.
es, _ /*err*/ = cli.Get(
  NewEmployeeQuery().TenureRankLte(5).Build(),
  shared.NewTemporalCoordinates(tt, vt))
for _, e := range NewEmployeeIterator(es).Items() {
  d, _ /*err*/ := cli.GetRef(e.Department())
  dep, _ /*ok*/ := d.(*Department)
  certIt, _ /*err*/ := cli.GetRefs(e.Certifications())
  certs := make([]string, 0)
  for _, c := range NewCertificationIterator(certIt).Items() {
    certs = append(certs, c.Name)
  }
  slog.Info("Employee",
    "FirstName", e.FirstName, "LastName", e.LastName,
    "TenureRank", e.TenureRank, "Department", dep.Name,
    "Certifications", strings.Join(certs, ","))
}
```

In addition to `Eq` ("equal to") and `Lte` ("less than or equal to"), we'll want `Gte` ("greater than or equal to"), along with the strict inequality versions, `Lt` ("less than") and `Gt` ("greater than"). We'll also want to be able to query *within* the list of `Certifications` so that we might find, say, all of the `Employees` who have the `cfa Certification`. In the next section, we'll see where those functions – along with the `Querys` and `Iterators` – come from.

Codegen(eration) example

The canonical example of code generation in Go is stringer, which generates a `String()` function for types like enums (`iotas`). Suppose we have the following:

```
type Day int

const (
  Mon Day = iota
  Tue
  Wed
  Thu
  Fri
  Sat
  Sun
)

func main() {
  fmt.Printf("%s", Mon)
}
```

As written, that code won't print the string `"Mon"`. Instead, it will print the string `"0"`! That's because we haven't given it a nice `String()` function yet, and that's what stringer does for us. In a separate file suffixed with "_string.go" by default, stringer will generate:

```
// Code generated by "stringer -type Day days.go"; DO NOT EDIT.

package main

import "strconv"

func _() {
  // An "invalid array index" compiler error signifies
  // that the constant values have changed.
  // Re-run the stringer command to generate them again.
  var x [1]struct{}
  _ = x[Mon-0]
  _ = x[Tue-1]
  _ = x[Wed-2]
  _ = x[Thu-3]
```

```
  _ = x[Fri-4]
  _ = x[Sat-5]
  _ = x[Sun-6]
}

const _Day_name = "MonTueWedThuFriSatSun"

var _Day_index = [...]uint8{0, 3, 6, 9, 12, 15, 18, 21}

func (i Day) String() string {
  if i < 0 || i >= Day(len(_Day_index)-1) {
    return "Day(" + strconv.FormatInt(int64(i), 10) + ")"
  }
  return _Day_name[_Day_index[i]:_Day_index[i+1]]
}
```

While that might look different from the naïve implementation, it does cause our original code to print the string `"Mon"` as we expect.

But how does it know the `strings` to generate? At the heart of the implementation is some code that parses the given file into an Abstract Syntax Tree, or AST. The AST is a tree representation of the source code, eliding syntactic elements like braces versus indentation to define scope. Nodes in the AST represent elements of the source code like objects or operations on objects. Go makes it easy to generate and analyze the AST of Go source code using the ast package, and we will use it to generate some functions that allow users to easily read and write their objects.

Raw Client functions

Since the `Client` will handle `BdObject`s and not the user's own classes, we refer to these as "raw" functions. Some may prefer the word "generic," but that is too easily confused with Go's generics, so we'll stick with "raw." Semantics aside, the generator will produce code for things like type assertions so that users can comfortably use their own types rather than `BdObject`s.

Let's look at the simplest function in the `Client`, `GetLsqt()`, which gets the `Lsqt` from the server. We will need a few things to get started. Since we have already defined `service Reader` in Chapter 2, we need only define the request and response objects, along with response types and error types:

```
// proto/server/reader/reader.proto

enum ReadResponseType {
  UNKNOWN = 0;
  SUCCESS = 1;
  FAIL = 2;
```

```
}

enum ReadResponseErrorType {
  UNKNOWN_ERROR = 0;
  INTERNAL = 1;
  BAD_REQUEST = 2;
  FUTURE_TT = 3;
}

message ReadLsqtRequest {}

message ReadLsqtResponse {
  ReadResponseType response_type = 1;
  int64 lsqt = 2;
}
```

The behavior of the messages is probably obvious: we send a `ReadLsqtRequest`
with no fields, and we receive a `ReadLsqtResponse` with a response type that tells
us whether or not the request was successful. If it was, then we also receive the
`Lsqt` as an `int64`. The `Client` implementation, therefore, is mostly some error
handling and type instantiation. Note that `ReadLsqtResponse` doesn't include an
error type because only the equivalent of an `INTERNAL` error could cause it to fail.

```
// client/impl/client.go

func (c *Client) GetLsqt() (shared.Tt, error) {
  req := &readerp.ReadLsqtRequest{}
  resp, err := c.readerClient.ReadLsqt(c.ctx, req)
  if err != nil {
    return shared.Tt(-1), err
  }
  if resp.ResponseType != readerp.ReadResponseType_SUCCESS {
    return shared.Tt(-1),
      fmt.Errorf(
        "Request failed: %s", resp.ResponseType.String())
  }
  return shared.Tt(resp.Lsqt), nil
}
```

Now that we can get the `Lsqt`, we can implement `CatchUp()`, which will allow us
to wait a finite amount of time for the server to catch up to our write(s). We'll
`GetLsqt()` every `catchUpMillis` milliseconds until either the `Lsqt` has advanced
at least as far as the given `tt`, or we have waited at least the given `waitMillis`,
after which we'll give up:

```
// client/impl/client.go

func (c *Client) CatchUp(
```

```
  tt shared.Tt,
  waitMillis int,
) (shared.Tt, error) {
  ticker := time.NewTicker(catchUpMillis * time.Millisecond)
  done := time.After(time.Duration(waitMillis) *
time.Millisecond)
  for {
    select {
    case <-ticker.C:
      curTt, err := c.GetLsqt()
      if err != nil {
        return shared.Tt(-1), err
      }
      if curTt.Equal(tt) || curTt.After(tt) {
        return curTt, nil
      }
    case <-done:
      ticker.Stop()
      return shared.Tt(-1), fmt.Errorf("Failed to catch up")
    }
  }
}
```

Now it's time to read an object. We have a message for both the request and the response, and each unsuccessful response will have an error type:

```
// proto/server/reader/reader.proto

message ReadRequest {
  enum ReadRequestType {
    UNKNOWN = 0;
    READ_INDEX_CONDITIONS = 1;
    READ_PREVIOUS = 2;
  }

  // index_conditions are ANDed together, so only objects that
  // match all of the conditions will be returned.
  ReadRequestType request_type = 1;
  repeated index.IndexCondition index_conditions = 2;
  int64 tt = 3;
  int64 vt = 4;
  string ts_id = 5;
}

message ReadResponse {
  message ReadObject {
    string object_id = 1;
    string fqn = 2;
    bytes attrs = 3;
```

```
    // If is_tombstone == true, then even though we'll get an
    // empty blob in the client, there's really no data. This
    // can happen on queries where the object_id is found,
    // but the query is in a deleted rectangle.
    bool is_tombstone = 4;
    int64 last_write = 5;
    int64 tt_from = 6;
    int64 vt_from = 7;
    int64 tt_resolved_at = 8;
    int64 vt_resolved_at = 9;
    string ts_id = 10;
  }
  ReadResponseType response_type = 1;
  ReadResponseErrorType response_error_type = 2;
  repeated ReadObject read_objects = 3;
}
```

For a simple object read, we won't need all of those fields. Most of the interesting work will be done in the `IndexConditions()` function that we'll generate later in the chapter. One thing we still need to fill in is `index.IndexCondition`. This will be both how we send indexed fields from the client to the server and how we read objects by indexed fields. First, we'll want some operations like "greater than," "less than," and so forth:

```
// proto/server/index/index.proto

enum IndexConditionOp {
  UNKNOWN = 0;
  EQUAL = 1;
  GREATER_THAN = 2;
  GREATER_THAN_OR_EQUAL_TO = 3;
  LESS_THAN = 4;
  LESS_THAN_OR_EQUAL_TO = 5;
  IN = 6;
}
```

Then, we'll want the actual structure of `index.IndexConditions`:

```
// proto/server/index/index.proto

message IndexCondition {
  string key = 1;
  IndexConditionOp op = 2;
  // Set these if the corresponding _value is set. Otherwise,
  // e.g., GetBoolValue() == false doesn't tell us whether or
  // not the field was set or if it's the default value.
  bool is_object_id_value = 3;
  bool is_fqn_value = 5;
```

```
  bool is_bool_value = 7;
  bool is_int32_value = 9;
  bool is_int64_value = 11;
  bool is_uint32_value = 13;
  bool is_uint64_value = 15;
  bool is_float_value = 17;
  bool is_double_value = 19;
  bool is_string_value = 21;
  oneof value {
    string object_id_value = 4;
    string fqn_value = 6;
    bool bool_value = 8;
    int32 int32_value = 10;
    int64 int64_value = 12;
    uint32 uint32_value = 14;
    uint64 uint64_value = 16;
    float float_value = 18;
    double double_value = 20;
    string string_value = 22;
  }
  repeated string object_ids = 23;
  bool is_key = 24;
  bool is_unique = 25;
}
```

It may be obvious from looking at the fields above that Go and protobuf have different data types, so we'll need to map Go's types to protobuf's types. We'll use the following mapping:

Go type(s)	Protobuf type
`bool`	`bool`
`int, int8, int16, int32`	`int32`
`int64`	`int64`
`uint, uint8, uint16, uint32`	`uint32`
`uint64`	`uint64`
`float32`	`float`
`float64`	`double`
`string`	`string`
`complex64, complex128, error`	`bytes`

`ObjectId` and `Fqn` will both be treated as `string`. `complex64`, `complex128`, and `error` will use types called `PersistableComplex64`, `PersistableComplex128`, and `PersistableError`, respectively, and be serialized to `bytes`.

With that structure in place, we have enough to send a read request from the client to the server:

```
// client/impl/client.go

func (c *Client) Get(
  iq *cshared.IndexedQuery,
  tc *shared.TemporalCoordinates,
) (*cshared.BdObjectIterator, error) {
  req := &readerp.ReadRequest{
    RequestType:     readerp.ReadRequest_READ_INDEX_CONDITIONS,
    IndexConditions: iq.IndexConditions(),
    Tt:              int64(tc.Tt),
    Vt:              int64(tc.Vt),
  }
  return c.readFromClient(req)
}
```

The helper function `readFromClient()` simply converts `ReadObject`s in the `ReadResponse` into `BdObjectI`s:

```
// client/impl/client.go

func (c *Client) readFromClient(
  req *readerp.ReadRequest,
) (*cshared.BdObjectIterator, error) {
  resp, err := c.readerClient.Read(c.ctx, req)
  if err != nil {
    return nil, err
  }
  if resp.ResponseType != readerp.ReadResponseType_SUCCESS {
    return nil,
      fmt.Errorf(
        "Request failed: %s", resp.ResponseErrorType.String())
  }
  objs := make([]*cshared.BdObject, len(resp.ReadObjects))
  for idx, ro := range resp.ReadObjects {
    objs[idx] = cshared.NewBdObject(
      shared.ObjectId(ro.ObjectId), shared.Fqn(ro.Fqn),
      ro.Attrs, ro.IsTombstone, shared.Tt(ro.LastWrite),
      shared.Tt(ro.TtFrom), shared.Vt(ro.VtFrom),
      shared.Tt(ro.TtResolvedAt), shared.Vt(ro.VtResolvedAt),
      shared.TsId(ro.TsId))
  }
  it := cshared.NewBdObjectIterator(objs)
  return it, nil
}
```

Suppose we have a version of an object that was created by RESTORE. We can easily read the previous version. Notice that instead of using READ_INDEX_CONDITIONS as the RequestType, we'll use READ_PREVIOUS.

```
// client/impl/client.go
```

```
func (c *Client) GetPrevious(
  bobj cshared.BdObjectI,
) (*cshared.BdObjectIterator, error) {
  if bobj.TsId().IsNil() {
    return nil, nil
  }
  req := &readerp.ReadRequest{
    RequestType: readerp.ReadRequest_READ_PREVIOUS,
    TsId:        string(bobj.TsId()),
  }
  return c.readFromClient(req)
}
```

If an object refers to another object via a "ref" tag, we can retrieve it by piggy-backing on Get() and passing specially crafted indexes for the ObjectId and the Fqn of the referenced object:

```
// client/impl/client.go

func (c *Client) GetRef(
  r *cshared.RefMeta,
) (cshared.BdObjectI, error) {
  if r == nil {
    return nil, nil
  }
  iq := cshared.NewIndexedQuery().
    AddIndexCondition(&indexp.IndexCondition{
      Key:              shared.ObjectIdKey,
      Op:               indexp.IndexConditionOp_EQUAL,
      IsObjectIdValue: true,
      Value: &indexp.IndexCondition_ObjectIdValue{
        ObjectIdValue: string(r.ObjectId),
      },
    }).AddIndexCondition(&indexp.IndexCondition{
      Key:        shared.FqnKey,
      Op:         indexp.IndexConditionOp_EQUAL,
      IsFqnValue: true,
      Value: &indexp.IndexCondition_FqnValue{
        FqnValue: string(r.Fqn),
      },
    })
  it, err := c.Get(iq, r.TemporalCoordinates)
  if err != nil {
    return nil, err
  }
  return r.F(it), nil
}
```

If the `r.F(it)` is confusing, don't worry: we'll generate it later in this chapter. For now, just know that it is a function to convert from a `BdObjectI` returned by `Get()` to the correct type.

`GetRefs()` is similar but returns a slice of referenced objects rather than a single object:

```
// client/impl/client.go

func (c *Client) GetRefs(
  r *cshared.RefMeta,
) (*cshared.BdObjectIterator, error) {
  if r == nil {
    return cshared.NewBdObjectIterator(
      make([]*cshared.BdObject, 0)), nil
  }
  oids := make([]string, len(r.ObjectIds))
  for i, oid := range r.ObjectIds {
    oids[i] = string(oid)
  }
  iq := cshared.NewIndexedQuery().
    AddIndexCondition(&indexp.IndexCondition{
      Key:       shared.ObjectIdKey,
      Op:        indexp.IndexConditionOp_IN,
      ObjectIds: oids,
    })
  req := &readerp.ReadRequest{
    RequestType:     readerp.ReadRequest_READ_INDEX_CONDITIONS,
    IndexConditions: iq.IndexConditions(),
    Tt:              int64(r.TemporalCoordinates.Tt),
    Vt:              int64(r.TemporalCoordinates.Vt),
  }
  return c.readFromClient(req)
}
```

Let's now turn our attention to writes. Like reads, writes will have a message type for requests and a message type for responses, along with response types and response error types. Notice that the error types are familiar from Chapter 5.

```
// proto/server/writer/writer.proto

enum WriteResponseType {
  UNKNOWN = 0;
  SUCCESS = 1;
  FAIL = 2;
}

enum WriteResponseErrorType {
  UNKNOWN_ERROR = 0;
```

```
  INTERNAL = 1;
  CONFLICT = 2;
  STALE = 3;
  BAD_REQUEST = 4;
  UNFULL = 5;
  KEY_CONSTRAINT = 6;
  IMPERMANENT_KEY = 7;
  UNIQUE_CONSTRAINT = 8;
}
```

The request and response message types are straightforward:

```
// proto/server/writer/writer.proto

message WriteRequest {
  enum WriteRequestType {
    UNKNOWN = 0;
    PUT = 1;
    DELETE = 2;
    RESTORE = 3;
  }

  message WriteObject {
    string object_id = 1;
    string fqn = 2;
    int64 last_read = 3;
    int64 vt_from = 4;
    bytes attrs = 5;
    repeated index.IndexCondition index_conditions = 6;
    string ts_id = 7;
  }

  WriteRequestType request_type = 1;
  repeated WriteObject write_objects = 2;
}

message WriteResponse {
  WriteResponseType response_type = 1;
  WriteResponseErrorType response_error_type = 2;
  int64 tt = 3;
}
```

Though there are three kinds of writes – PUT, DELETE, and RESTORE – they are
similar enough that we use a single function to build a write request for all of them:

```
// client/impl/client.go

func (c *Client) buildWriteRequest(
```

```
    bobjs []cshared.BdObjectI,
    vt shared.Vt,
    reqType writerp.WriteRequest_WriteRequestType,
) (*writerp.WriteRequest, error) {
    writeObjects :=
      make([]*writerp.WriteRequest_WriteObject, len(bobjs))
    for i, bobj := range bobjs {
      if hv, ok := bobj.(cshared.HasValidator); ok {
        if err := hv.Validate(); err != nil {
          slog.Error("buildWriteRequest()",
            "bobj", bobj, "err", err.Error())
          return nil, err
        }
      }
      writeObjects[i] = &writerp.WriteRequest_WriteObject{
        ObjectId:        string(bobj.ObjectId()),
        Fqn:             string(bobj.Fqn()),
        LastRead:        int64(bobj.LastRead()),
        IndexConditions: bobj.IndexConditions(),
        VtFrom:          int64(vt),
      }
      if reqType == writerp.WriteRequest_PUT {
        data, err := bobj.ToJson()
        if err != nil {
          log.Default().Fatal("Failed to marshal", "bobj", bobj)
          return nil, err
        }
        writeObjects[i].Attrs = data
      } else if reqType == writerp.WriteRequest_RESTORE {
        writeObjects[i].TsId = string(bobj.TsId())
      }
    }
    return &writerp.WriteRequest{
      RequestType:  reqType,
      WriteObjects: writeObjects,
    }, nil
}
```

Now that we can assemble a write request, we need to be able to send it and to process the response:

```
// client/impl/client.go

func (c *Client) doWriteRequest(
  req *writerp.WriteRequest,
) (shared.Tt, error) {
  resp, err := c.writerClient.Write(c.ctx, req)
  if err != nil {
    return shared.Tt(-1), err
  }
  if resp.ResponseType != writerp.WriteResponseType_SUCCESS {
```

```
    return shared.Tt(-1),
      fmt.Errorf(
        "Request failed: %s", resp.ResponseErrorType.String())
  }
  return shared.Tt(resp.Tt), nil
}
```

With those two pieces, `Put()` – and its companion, `MultiPut()` – are very simple:

```
// client/impl/client.go

func (c *Client) Put(
  bobj cshared.BdObjectI,
  vt shared.Vt,
) (shared.Tt, error) {
  return c.MultiPut([]cshared.BdObjectI{bobj}, vt)
}

func (c *Client) MultiPut(
  bobjs []cshared.BdObjectI,
  vt shared.Vt,
) (shared.Tt, error) {
  req, err :=
    c.buildWriteRequest(bobjs, vt, writerp.WriteRequest_PUT)
  if err != nil {
    return shared.Tt(-1), err
  }
  return c.doWriteRequest(req)
}
```

`Delete()` and `MultiDelete()` are practically identical:

```
// client/impl/client.go

func (c *Client) Delete(
  bobj cshared.BdObjectI,
  vt shared.Vt,
) (shared.Tt, error) {
  return c.MultiDelete([]cshared.BdObjectI{bobj}, vt)
}

func (c *Client) MultiDelete(
  bobjs []cshared.BdObjectI,
  vt shared.Vt,
) (shared.Tt, error) {
  req, err :=
    c.buildWriteRequest(bobjs, vt, writerp.WriteRequest_DELETE)
  if err != nil {
    return shared.Tt(-1), err
  }
  return c.doWriteRequest(req)
```

```
}
```

As are `Restore()` and `MultiRestore()`:

```go
// client/impl/client.go

func (c *Client) Restore(
  bobj cshared.BdObjectI,
  vt shared.Vt,
) (shared.Tt, error) {
  return c.MultiRestore([]cshared.BdObjectI{bobj}, vt)
}

func (c *Client) MultiRestore(
  bobjs []cshared.BdObjectI,
  vt shared.Vt,
) (shared.Tt, error) {
  req, err :=
    c.buildWriteRequest(bobjs, vt,
writerp.WriteRequest_RESTORE)
  if err != nil {
    return shared.Tt(-1), err
  }
  return c.doWriteRequest(req)
}
```

That's all of the behavior that we need in our client! In Chapter 10, we'll look at the generator, which will allow us to generate code using only struct tags. The generated code will call the raw client methods that we've written in this chapter, making it easy to write idiomatic code with existing models.

Chapter 10: Generator

Let's take a look at the generator, which will use a `switch` on different `ast` types to populate a list of fields on a given `struct`. Once it has finished parsing the AST, it will render the generated code using a template. Fortunately, text/template, part of the Go standard library, provides simple, familiar constructs like loops to make this a breeze. First, let's look at the template to see how the functions will look. Once we know what we need to generate, we'll know what data we need to collect.

First, let's look at the basics: we're abiding by our interface `BdObjectI`, and we have two simple constructors. The first generates an `ObjectId` automatically, and the second takes an `ObjectId`.

```
// gen/lib/template.go

package {{ .PackageName }}

{{ range $strct := .Structs -}}
var _ cshared.BdObjectI = &{{ .Name }}{}
var {{ .Name }}Fqn = shared.FqnOf(&{{ .Name }}{})

func New{{ .Name }}({{ range $field := .Fields }}
  {{ .ParamName }} {{ if .IsPointer -}}
{{ if not .IsContainer }}*{{ end }}{{ end }}{{ .Type }},
{{- end }}
)  *{{ .Name }} {
  return New{{ .Name }}WithObjectId({{ range $field := .Fields }}
    {{ .ParamName}},
  {{- end }}
  shared.NewObjectId())
}

func New{{ .Name }}WithObjectId({{ range $field := .Fields }}
  _{{ .ParamName }} {{ if .IsPointer -}}
{{ if not .IsContainer }}*{{ end }}{{ end }}{{ .Type }},
{{- end }}
  oid shared.ObjectId,
)  *{{ .Name }} {
  e := &{{ .Name }}{ {{ range $field := .Fields }}
    {{ .Name }}: _{{ .ParamName }},
  {{- end }}
  }
  e.SetObjectId(oid)
  e.SetFqn({{ .Name}}Fqn)
  return e
}
```

Astute readers will notice that _{{ .ParamName }} is prefixed with an underscore. This prevents the case of a field named e colliding with e := ... corresponding to the new object that we are creating.

From our Employee example earlier in the chapter, here are the generated constructors:

```
var EmployeeFqn = shared.FqnOf(&Employee{})

func NewEmployee(
  id int,
  firstName string,
  lastName string,
  tenureRank int,
  _department *Department,
  _certifications []*Certification,
) *Employee {
  return NewEmployeeWithObjectId(
    id,
    firstName,
    lastName,
    tenureRank,
    _department,
    _certifications,
    shared.NewObjectId())
}

func NewEmployeeWithObjectId(
  _id int,
  _firstName string,
  _lastName string,
  _tenureRank int,
  __department *Department,
  __certifications []*Certification,
  oid shared.ObjectId,
) *Employee {
  e := &Employee{
    Id:               _id,
    FirstName:        _firstName,
    LastName:         _lastName,
    TenureRank:       _tenureRank,
    _department:      __department,
    _certifications:  __certifications,
  }
  e.SetObjectId(oid)
  e.SetFqn(EmployeeFqn)
  return e
}
```

Next, we'll add a function to convert the object to JSON, which will be the representation that we convert to a byte array to store in the `AttrStore`:

```
// gen/lib/template.go

func (e *{{ .Name }}) ToJson() ([]byte, error) {
  return json.Marshal(struct {
    ObjectId shared.ObjectId
    Fqn       shared.Fqn
    {{ range $field := .Fields -}}
      {{ if .Tags.IsRef -}}
    {{ .TitleName }} shared.ObjectId ` +
  "`json:\"_{{ .TitleName }}Ref,omitempty\"`" + `
      {{ else if .Tags.IsRefs -}}
    {{ .TitleName }} []shared.ObjectId ` +
  "`json:\"_{{ .TitleName }}Refs,omitempty\"`" + `
      {{ else -}}
    {{ .TitleName }} {{ if .IsPointer }}*{{ end -}}
{{ if .TransformedType }}*{{ .TransformedType }}{{ else -}}
{{ .Type }}{{ end }}
      {{ end -}}
    {{ end -}}
  }{
    ObjectId:    e.ObjectId(),
    Fqn:          e.Fqn(),
    {{ range $field := .Fields -}}
      {{ if .Tags.IsRef -}}
    {{ .TitleName }}: e.{{ .Name }}ObjectId(),
      {{ else if .Tags.IsRefs -}}
    {{ .TitleName }}: e.{{ .Name }}ObjectIds(),
      {{ else -}}
    {{ .TitleName }}: {{ if .TransformedType -}}
&{{ .TransformedType }}{ e.{{ .TitleName }} }{{ else -}}
e.{{ .TitleName }}{{ end }},
      {{ end -}}
    {{ end -}}
  })
}
```

`Employee.ToJson()` **then looks like this:**

```
func (e *Employee) ToJson() ([]byte, error) {
  return json.Marshal(struct {
    ObjectId      shared.ObjectId
    Fqn           shared.Fqn
    Id            int
    FirstName     string
    LastName      string
```

```
        TenureRank       int
        Department       shared.ObjectId
          `json:"_DepartmentRef,omitempty"`
        Certifications []shared.ObjectId
          `json:"_CertificationsRefs,omitempty"`
    }{
      ObjectId:        e.ObjectId(),
      Fqn:             e.Fqn(),
      Id:              e.Id,
      FirstName:       e.FirstName,
      LastName:        e.LastName,
      TenureRank:      e.TenureRank,
      Department:      e._departmentObjectId(),
      Certifications: e._certificationsObjectIds(),
    })
}
```

`IndexConditions()` generates the index entries for the object. These will be sent to the server on write requests:

```
// gen/lib/template.go

func (e *{{ .Name }}) IndexConditions() []*indexp.IndexCondition {
  ics := []*indexp.IndexCondition{
    {{ range $field := .Fields }}{{ if .Tags.IsIndexed -}}
    &indexp.IndexCondition{
      Key:                    "{{ .Name }}",
      Op:                     indexp.IndexConditionOp_EQUAL,
      Is{{ .IndexType }}Value: true,
      Value:
        &indexp.IndexCondition_{{ .IndexType }}Value{
          {{ .IndexType }}Value: {{ .EDotNameWithExtractor }},
        },
      {{ if .Tags.IsKey }}IsKey:       true,{{ end }}
      {{ if .Tags.IsUnique }}IsUnique: true,{{ end }}
    },
    {{ end }}{{ end -}}
  }
  {{ range $field := .Fields }}{{ if .Tags.IsRef -}}
  if e.{{ .Name }} != nil && !e.{{ .Name }}.ObjectId().IsNil() {
    ics = append(ics, &indexp.IndexCondition{
      Key:            "_{{ .TitleName }}Ref",
      Op:             indexp.IndexConditionOp_EQUAL,
      IsObjectIdValue: true,
      Value:          &indexp.IndexCondition_ObjectIdValue{
        ObjectIdValue: string(e.{{ .Name }}.ObjectId()),
      },
    })
  }
```

```
  {{ else if .Tags.IsRefs -}}
oids{{ .TitleName }}Refs :=
  make([]string, len(e.{{ .Name }}ObjectIds()))
for i, oid := range e.{{ .Name }}ObjectIds() {
  oids{{ .TitleName }}Refs[i] = string(oid)
}
ics = append(ics, &indexp.IndexCondition{
  Key:        "_{{ .TitleName }}Refs",
  Op:         indexp.IndexConditionOp_IN,
  ObjectIds: oids{{ .TitleName }}Refs,
})
{{ end }}{{ end -}}
return ics
}
```

Note the use of the underscore in the naming of `_DepartmentRef` and in `_CertificationsRefs` in `Employee.IndexConditions()`. The former will be zero or one `ObjectIds`, and the latter will be zero or more `ObjectIds`. We are able to `Marshal()` those using our anonymous struct with the tags `` `json:"_{{ .TitleName }}Ref,omitempty"` `` and `` `json:"_{{ .TitleName }}Refs,omitempty"` ``.

Because this particular example is so long, we break it into two parts here. The first part (below) is the set of non-reference values.

```
func (e *Employee) IndexConditions() []*indexp.IndexCondition {
  ics := []*indexp.IndexCondition{
    {
      Key:          "Id",
      Op:           indexp.IndexConditionOp_EQUAL,
      IsInt32Value: true,
      Value: &indexp.IndexCondition_Int32Value{
        Int32Value: int32(e.Id),
      },
      IsKey: true,
    },
    {
      Key:           "LastName",
      Op:            indexp.IndexConditionOp_EQUAL,
      IsStringValue: true,
      Value: &indexp.IndexCondition_StringValue{
        StringValue: e.LastName,
      },
    },
    {
      Key:          "TenureRank",
      Op:           indexp.IndexConditionOp_EQUAL,
      IsInt32Value: true,
      Value: &indexp.IndexCondition_Int32Value{
```

```
          Int32Value: int32(e.TenureRank),
        },

        IsUnique: true,
      },
    }
    ...
}
```

The second part of the function handles references:

```
  ...
  if e._department != nil && !e._department.ObjectId().IsNil()
{
    ics = append(ics, &indexp.IndexCondition{
      Key:               "_DepartmentRef",
      Op:                indexp.IndexConditionOp_EQUAL,
      IsObjectIdValue: true,
      Value: &indexp.IndexCondition_ObjectIdValue{
        ObjectIdValue: string(e._department.ObjectId()),
      },
    })
  }
  oidsCertificationsRefs :=
    make([]string, len(e._certificationsObjectIds()))
  for i, oid := range e._certificationsObjectIds() {
    oidsCertificationsRefs[i] = string(oid)
  }
  ics = append(ics, &indexp.IndexCondition{
    Key:        "_CertificationsRefs",
    Op:         indexp.IndexConditionOp_IN,
    ObjectIds: oidsCertificationsRefs,
  })
  return ics
  ...
```

If you squint, you can probably see that we're going to need to call `{{ .Name }}ObjectId()` (and the plural form). That handles references and is generated next (ranging over every field, of course):

```
// gen/lib/template.go

{{ if .Tags.IsRef -}}
func (e *{{ $strct.Name }}) {{ .Name }}ObjectId() shared.ObjectId {
  if e.{{ .Name }} == nil {
    return shared.ObjectId("")
  }
  return e.{{ .Name }}.ObjectId()
}
```

```
func (e *{{ $strct.Name }}) Set{{ .TitleName }}(
  o {{ if .IsPointer }}*{{ end }}{{ .Type }},
) {
  e.{{ .Name }} = o
}
{{ end }}


// gen/lib/template.go

{{ if .Tags.IsRefs -}}
func (e *{{ $strct.Name }}) {{ .Name }}ObjectIds(
) []shared.ObjectId {
  a := make([]shared.ObjectId, len(e.{{ .Name }}))
  for i, o := range e.{{ .Name }} {
    a[i] = o.ObjectId()
  }
  return a
}


func (e *{{ $strct.Name }}) Set{{ .TitleName }}(o {{ .Type }}) {
  e.{{ .Name }} = o
}
{{ end }}
```

For the `Employee` references, note that we also generate setters:

```
func (e *Employee) _departmentObjectId() shared.ObjectId {
  if e._department == nil {
    return shared.ObjectId("")
  }
  return e._department.ObjectId()
}


func (e *Employee) SetDepartment(
  o *Department,
) {
  e._department = o
}
```

And for a slice of references:

```
// gen/lib/template.go

func (e *Employee) _certificationsObjectIds() []shared.ObjectId {
  a := make([]shared.ObjectId, len(e._certifications))
  for i, o := range e._certifications {
    a[i] = o.ObjectId()
  }
  return a
```

```
}

func (e *Employee) SetCertifications(o []*Certification) {
  e._certifications = o
}

func (e *Employee) _certificationsObjectIds() []shared.ObjectId
{
  a := make([]shared.ObjectId, len(e._certifications))
  for i, o := range e._certifications {
    a[i] = o.ObjectId()
  }
  return a
}

func (e *Employee) SetCertifications(o []*Certification) {
  e._certifications = o
}
```

To fetch references, we'll use a `struct` called `RefMeta`:

```
// client/shared/ref_meta.go

type RefMeta struct {
  Fqn                 gshared.Fqn
  ObjectId            gshared.ObjectId
  ObjectIds           []gshared.ObjectId
  TemporalCoordinates *gshared.TemporalCoordinates
  F                   func(*BdObjectIterator) BdObjectI
}
```

And, we'll generate appropriate methods to produce `RefMeta`:

```
// gen/lib/template.go

{{ if or .Tags.IsRef .Tags.IsRefs -}}
func (e *{{ $strct.Name }}) {{ .TitleName }}() *cshared.RefMeta {
  if e.{{ .Name }} == nil {
    return nil
  }
  return &cshared.RefMeta{
    TemporalCoordinates: shared.NewTemporalCoordinates(
      e.TtResolvedAt(), e.VtResolvedAt()),
  {{ if .Tags.IsRef -}}
    Fqn: {{ .TitleName }}Fqn,
    ObjectId: e.{{ .Name }}.ObjectId(),
    F: func(b *cshared.BdObjectIterator) cshared.BdObjectI {
      return New{{ .TitleName }}Iterator(b).First()
    },
  {{ else -}}
```

```
    Fqn: {{ .Tags.RefsType }}Fqn,
    ObjectIds: e.{{ .Name }}ObjectIds(),
  {{ end -}}
  }
}
{{ end -}}
```

For both `Employee.Department()` and `Employee.Certifications()`:

```
func (e *Employee) Department() *cshared.RefMeta {
  if e._department == nil {
    return nil
  }
  return &cshared.RefMeta{
    TemporalCoordinates: shared.NewTemporalCoordinates(
      e.TtResolvedAt(), e.VtResolvedAt()),
    Fqn:       DepartmentFqn,
    ObjectId: e._department.ObjectId(),
    F: func(b *cshared.BdObjectIterator) cshared.BdObjectI {
      return NewDepartmentIterator(b).First()
    },
  }
}

func (e *Employee) Certifications() *cshared.RefMeta {
  if e._certifications == nil {
    return nil
  }
  return &cshared.RefMeta{
    TemporalCoordinates: shared.NewTemporalCoordinates(
      e.TtResolvedAt(), e.VtResolvedAt()),
    Fqn:       CertificationFqn,
    ObjectIds: e._certificationsObjectIds(),
  }
}
```

Notice `r.F` in `Department()`: this was mentioned earlier in the chapter and does precisely the type coercion that we need!

Before we move on, notice one more subtle detail: the `TemporalCoordinates` of the `RefMeta` – and therefore, the `TemporalCoordinates` at which we load the corresponding objects – is (`TtResolvedAt()`, `VtResolvedAt()`). This means that referenced objects are loaded at the same `TemporalCoordinates` as the referring object. Even though we know that the referring object exists there – we just loaded it, after all – there is no guarantee that the referenced objects exist there since the objects have independent lifecycles.

And finally, we arrive at the query machinery. The central query object will be a {{ .Name }}Query. The {{ .Name }}Query will have a fluent API, allowing us to write expressions like `q.WhereXEq(1).WhereYEq(2)` to mean "(the existing query) AND (x == 1) AND (x == 2)." We won't generate functions for `OR`; users must manually combine collections of objects if they wish to use `OR` logic. Adding such logic would be an interesting extension for use cases in which `OR` logic is required.

We'll generate the `{{ .Name }}Query`struct, a constructor, and a `Build()` function that simply returns the `IndexedQuery`:

```
// gen/lib/template.go

type {{ .Name }}Query struct {
  q *cshared.IndexedQuery
}

func New{{ .Name }}Query() *{{ .Name }}Query {
  q := cshared.NewIndexedQuery().
    AddIndexCondition(&indexp.IndexCondition{
    Key: shared.FqnKey,
    Op: indexp.IndexConditionOp_EQUAL,
    IsFqnValue: true,
    Value: &indexp.IndexCondition_FqnValue{
      FqnValue: string({{ .Name }}Fqn),
    },
  })
  return &{{ .Name }}Query{
    q: q,
  }
}

func (eq *{{ .Name }}Query) Build() *cshared.IndexedQuery {
  return eq.q
}
```

These are trivial for `Employee` (and for other types, too):

```
type EmployeeQuery struct {
  q *cshared.IndexedQuery
}

func NewEmployeeQuery() *EmployeeQuery {
  q := cshared.NewIndexedQuery().
    AddIndexCondition(&indexp.IndexCondition{
      Key:        shared.FqnKey,
      Op:         indexp.IndexConditionOp_EQUAL,
      IsFqnValue: true,
      Value: &indexp.IndexCondition_FqnValue{
        FqnValue: string(EmployeeFqn),
```

```
    },
  })
  return &EmployeeQuery{
    q: q,
  }
}
```

Let's add a function to query by the obvious: `ObjectId`!

```
// gen/lib/template.go

func (eq *{{ $strct.Name }}Query) ObjectIdEq(
  oid shared.ObjectId,
) *{{ $strct.Name }}Query {
  eq.q.AddIndexCondition(&indexp.IndexCondition{
    Key:            "ObjectId",
    Op:             indexp.IndexConditionOp_EQUAL,
    IsObjectIdValue: true,
    Value:          &indexp.IndexCondition_ObjectIdValue{
      ObjectIdValue: string(oid),
    },
  })
  return eq
}

func (eq *EmployeeQuery) Build() *cshared.IndexedQuery {
  return eq.q
}

func (eq *EmployeeQuery) ObjectIdEq(
  oid shared.ObjectId,
) *EmployeeQuery {
  eq.q.AddIndexCondition(&indexp.IndexCondition{
    Key:            "ObjectId",
    Op:             indexp.IndexConditionOp_EQUAL,
    IsObjectIdValue: true,
    Value: &indexp.IndexCondition_ObjectIdValue{
      ObjectIdValue: string(oid),
    },
  })
  return eq
}
```

For every type of indexed field, we'll generate a helper function. For example, if any indexed fields are of type `string`, we'll generate `bdStringQueryHelper()` to avoid some boilerplate in cases where there is more than one indexed field of type `string`.

```
// gen/lib/template.go
```

```
{{ range $tipe, $sTipeIType := .FieldTypes -}}
{{ $iType := $sTipeIType.IndexType -}}
func (eq *{{ $strct.Name }}Query) bd{{ $iType }}QueryHelper(
  key string,
  value {{ $tipe }},
  op indexp.IndexConditionOp,
) *{{ $strct.Name}}Query {
  eq.q.AddIndexCondition(&indexp.IndexCondition{
    Key: key,
    Op: op,
    Is{{ $sTipeIType.IndexType }}Value: true,
    Value:
      &indexp.IndexCondition_{{ $iType }}Value{
      {{ $sTipeIType.IndexType }}Value: {{ .ValueWithExtractor }},
    },
  })
  return eq
}

{{ end -}}
```

We won't show all of the helper functions for querying by a type since they're so repetitive, but here's the one for querying by `int32`:

```
func (eq *EmployeeQuery) bdInt32QueryHelper(
  key string,
  value int,
  op indexp.IndexConditionOp,
) *EmployeeQuery {
  eq.q.AddIndexCondition(&indexp.IndexCondition{
    Key:           key,
    Op:            op,
    IsInt32Value: true,
    Value: &indexp.IndexCondition_Int32Value{
      Int32Value: int32(value),
    },
  })
  return eq
}
```

For every field, we'll generate filter functions that add to the list of `IndexConditions` to be sent to the server's `IndexStore`. Here's the template for `ref` and `refs`:

```
// gen/lib/template.go

{{ range $field := .Fields -}}
  {{ if .Tags.IsRef }}
```

```
func (eq *{{ $strct.Name }}Query) {{ .TitleName }}Eq(
  {{ .ParamName }} *{{ .Type }},
) *{{ $strct.Name }}Query {
  eq.q.AddIndexCondition(&indexp.IndexCondition{
    Key:              "_{{ .TitleName }}Ref",
    Op:               indexp.IndexConditionOp_EQUAL,
    IsObjectIdValue: true,
    Value:            &indexp.IndexCondition_ObjectIdValue{
      ObjectIdValue: string({{ .ParamName }}.ObjectId()),
    },
  })
  return eq
}
  {{ end }}
  {{ if .Tags.IsRefs }}
func (eq *{{ $strct.Name}}Query) {{ $field.TitleName }}Contains(
  {{ $field.ParamName }} *{{ .Tags.RefsType }},
) *{{ $strct.Name }}Query {
  eq.q.AddIndexCondition(&indexp.IndexCondition{
    Key:        "_{{ .TitleName }}Refs",
    Op:         indexp.IndexConditionOp_IN,
    ObjectIds: []string{string({{ .ParamName }}.ObjectId())},
  })
  return eq
}
  {{ end }}

// ... (0)

  {{ end -}}
{{ end -}}
```

And here is an example of the generated code:

```
func (eq *EmployeeQuery) DepartmentEq(
  _department *Department,
) *EmployeeQuery {
  eq.q.AddIndexCondition(&indexp.IndexCondition{
    Key:              "_DepartmentRef",
    Op:               indexp.IndexConditionOp_EQUAL,
    IsObjectIdValue: true,
    Value: &indexp.IndexCondition_ObjectIdValue{
      ObjectIdValue: string(_department.ObjectId()),
    },
  })
  return eq
}

func (eq *EmployeeQuery) CertificationsContains(
```

```
  _certifications *Certification,
) *EmployeeQuery {
  eq.q.AddIndexCondition(&indexp.IndexCondition{
    Key:       "_CertificationsRefs",
    Op:        indexp.IndexConditionOp_IN,
    ObjectIds: []string{string(_certifications.ObjectId())},
  })
  return eq
}
```

Here is the template for primitive types:

```
// gen/lib/template.go

// ... (0)

  {{ if and .Tags.IsIndexed .CanIndex }}
func (eq *{{ $strct.Name }}Query) {{ .TitleName }}Eq(
  {{ .ParamName }} {{ .Type }},
) *{{ $strct.Name }}Query {
  return eq.bd{{ .SanitizedType }}QueryHelper(
    "{{ .Name }}",
    {{ if .Tags.IsRef -}}
    string({{ .ParamName }}.ObjectId()),
    {{ else -}}
    {{ .ParamName -}},
    {{ end }} indexp.IndexConditionOp_EQUAL)
}

    {{ if not .IsBool }}
      {{ range $methodKey, $opKey := $indexConditions -}}
      {{ $mk := $methodKey }}
func (eq *{{ $strct.Name }}Query) {{ $field.TitleName }}{{ $mk }}(
  {{ $field.ParamName }} {{ $field.Type }},
) *{{ $strct.Name }}Query {
  return eq.bd{{ $field.SanitizedType }}QueryHelper(
    "{{ $field.Name }}", {{ $field.ParamName }},
    indexp.IndexConditionOp_{{ $opKey }})
}
      {{ end }}
    {{ end }}
```

Again, there are many mostly repetitious functions, but here's the one for querying by Id equality:

```
func (eq *EmployeeQuery) IdEq(
  id int,
) *EmployeeQuery {
  return eq.bdInt32QueryHelper(
    "Id",
```

```
      id,
      indexp.IndexConditionOp_EQUAL)
}
```

In preparation for generating an `Iterator`, we need to handle unmarshalling, which will require an alias type to avoid infinite recursion. How might the infinite recursion happen? Consider an example without an alias type:

```
type Foo struct {
  A int
}

func (f *Foo) UnmarshalJSON(data []byte) error {
  return json.Unmarshal(data, f)
}

func main() {
  data := `{"A":1}`
  var f Foo
  json.Unmarshal([]byte(data), &f)
}
```

The call to `json.Unmarshal(data, f)` recursively calls `f.UnmarshalJSON(data)`, leading to an infinite loop.

```
// gen/lib/template.go

type bd{{ .Name }}UnmarshalAlias struct {
  cshared.BdObject
  {{ range $field := .Fields -}}
    {{ if .Tags.IsRef -}}
  {{ .TitleName }}Ref string ` +
  "`json:\"_{{ .TitleName }}Ref,omitempty\"`" + `
    {{ else if .Tags.IsRefs -}}
  {{ .TitleName }}Refs []shared.ObjectId ` +
  "`json:\"_{{ .TitleName }}Refs,omitempty\"`" + `
    {{ else -}}
  {{ .TitleName }} {{ if .TransformedType -}}
*{{ .TransformedType -}}
{{ else }}{{ if .IsPointer }}*{{ end }}{{ .Type }}{{ end }}
    {{ end -}}
  {{ end }}
}
```

The alias type that we generate for `Employee` is as follows:

```
type bdEmployeeUnmarshalAlias struct {
  cshared.BdObject
  Id                  int
```

```
  FirstName         string
  LastName          string
  TenureRank        int
  DepartmentRef     string
    `json:"_DepartmentRef,omitempty"`
  CertificationsRefs []shared.ObjectId
    `json:"_CertificationsRefs,omitempty"`
}
```

And `UnmarshalJSON()` itself:

```
// gen/lib/template.go

func (e *{{ .Name }}) UnmarshalJSON(data []byte) error {
  aux := &bd{{ .Name }}UnmarshalAlias{}
  if err := json.Unmarshal(data, aux); err != nil {
    return err
  }
  {{ range $field := .Fields -}}
    {{ if .Tags.IsRef -}}
  if !shared.ObjectId(aux.{{ .TitleName }}Ref).IsNil() {
    e.{{ .Name }} = &{{ .Type }}{}
    e.{{ .Name }}.SetObjectId(
      shared.ObjectId(aux.{{ .TitleName }}Ref))
  }
    {{ else if .Tags.IsRefs -}}
  if l := len(aux.{{ .TitleName }}Refs); l > 0 {
    e.{{ .Name }} = make([]*{{ .Tags.RefsType }}, l)
    for i, oid := range aux.{{ .TitleName }}Refs {
      e.{{ .Name }}[i] = &{{ .Tags.RefsType }}{}
      e.{{ .Name }}[i].SetObjectId(oid)
    }
  }
    {{ else -}}
  e.{{ .Name }} = aux.{{ .Name -}}
{{ if .TransformedType }}.Value().({{ .Type }}){{ end }}
    {{ end -}}
  {{ end -}}
  return nil
}
```

That produces `Employee.UnmarshalJSON()`:

```
func (e *Employee) UnmarshalJSON(data []byte) error {
  aux := &bdEmployeeUnmarshalAlias{}
  if err := json.Unmarshal(data, aux); err != nil {
    return err
  }
  e.Id = aux.Id
```

```
    e.FirstName = aux.FirstName
    e.LastName = aux.LastName
    e.TenureRank = aux.TenureRank
    if !shared.ObjectId(aux.DepartmentRef).IsNil() {
      e._department = &Department{}
      e._department.SetObjectId(
        shared.ObjectId(aux.DepartmentRef))
    }
    if l := len(aux.CertificationsRefs); l > 0 {
      e._certifications = make([]*Certification, l)
      for i, oid := range aux.CertificationsRefs {
        e._certifications[i] = &Certification{}
        e._certifications[i].SetObjectId(oid)
      }
    }
    return nil
}
```

Finally, we will generate the `{{ .Name }}Iterator` (and its constructor), which will take a `BdObjectIterator` of `BdObjectIs` and convert them to the correct type.

Why use an iterator rather than a method to convert, say, a slice of `BdObjectI`? We may want to implement server-side cursors providing zero or more results to the client on demand. Without knowing in advance how many results there might be, an iterator is an appropriate data structure to provide objects to a consumer.

```
// gen/lib/template.go

type {{ .Name }}Iterator struct {
  it func(yield func(int, *{{ .Name }})) bool)
}

func New{{ .Name }}Iterator(
  bobjIt *cshared.BdObjectIterator,
) *{{ .Name }}Iterator {
  return &{{ .Name }}Iterator{
    it: func(yield func(int, *{{ .Name }})) bool) {
      for idx, bobj := range bobjIt.Items() {
        obj := &{{ .Name }}{
          BdObject: *bobj,
        }
        err := json.Unmarshal([]byte(bobj.Data()), &obj)
        if err != nil {
          log.
            Default().
            Fatal("Failed to unmarshal {{ .Name }}",
              "err", err.Error(),
```

```
              "data", string(bobj.Data())))
        }
        if !yield(idx, obj) {
          return
        }
      }
    },
  }
}
```

The generated iterator for `Employee` is:

```
type EmployeeIterator struct {
  it func(yield func(int, *Employee) bool)
}

func NewEmployeeIterator(
  bobjIt *cshared.BdObjectIterator,
) *EmployeeIterator {
  return &EmployeeIterator{
    it: func(yield func(int, *Employee) bool) {
      for idx, bobj := range bobjIt.Items() {
        obj := &Employee{
          BdObject: *bobj,
        }
        err := json.Unmarshal([]byte(bobj.Data()), &obj)
        if err != nil {
          log.
            Default().
            Fatal("Failed to unmarshal Employee",
              "err", err.Error(),
              "data", string(bobj.Data())))
        }
        if !yield(idx, obj) {
          return
        }
      }
    },
  }
}
```

To get the items from the `{{ .Name }}Iterator`, we'll generate an `Items()`
method with the type assertion logic. The key is that `BdObjectI.Data()` provides
the JSON data to be unmarshaled into the `{{ .Name }}` class. Since we often want
a single element, such as in the case of a key or unique index lookup, we'll also
generate a `First()` function.

`// gen/lib/template.go`

```
func (eIt *{{ .Name }}Iterator) Items(
) iter.Seq2[int, *{{ .Name }}] {
  return eIt.it
}


func (eIt *{{ .Name }}Iterator) First() *{{ .Name }} {
  for _, bobj := range eIt.Items() {
    return bobj
  }
  return nil
}
```

And for `Employee`:

```
func (eIt *EmployeeIterator) Items() iter.Seq2[int, *Employee]
{
  return eIt.it
}

func (eIt *EmployeeIterator) First() *Employee {
  for _, bobj := range eIt.Items() {
    return bobj
  }
  return nil
}
```

Necessary data

Now that we know what we need to generate, we can create some `structs` to be populated with the requisite data as we walk the AST. In the previous section, we saw the following fields (such as `.Name`) that we'll need:

Field	Description
`.IndexConditions`	A `map[string]string` of pairs like `"Gt"` -> `"GREATER_THAN"`
`.PackageName`	The name of the package in which to generate the code
`.Structs`	The `structs` for which to generate the code

For each member of `.Structs`, we need to collect the following data:

Field	Description
`.Name`	The name of the `struct`, like `"Employee"`
`.Fields`	A list of the fields of the `struct`, along with some metadata about them
`.FieldTypes`	A deduplicated list of the types of each field in `.Fields`, along with some metadata about them

106

For each member of `.Fields`, we need to collect the following data:

Field	Description
`.Name`	The name of this field as the user defined it in the `struct`
`.ParamName`	The name of the parameter to use for this field in the function definitions
`.TitleName`	A pretty, titlecase version of `.Name`
`.ParamNameWithExtractor`	A string that, when evaluated, will return the value of this field coerced to `.IndexType`
`.EDotNameWithExtractor`	A string that, when evaluated, will return the value of `e.<this field>` coerced to `.IndexType`
`.Type`	The type of this field
`.TransformedType`	The type of this field that must be used in JSON marshal / unmarshal
`.IsPointer`	True if this field is a pointer type, false otherwise
`.IsContainer`	True if this field is a container type, false otherwise
`.IndexType`	The protobuf type to be used when indexing this type if `.IsIndexed`, blank otherwise
`.SanitizedType`	A string corresponding to `.IndexType` that can be safely included in the names of private functions
`.IsBool`	True if this field has type `bool`, false otherwise
`.CanIndex`	True if the type of this field can be indexed by this database, false otherwise
`.mt`	A (possibly `nil`) pointer to an instance of `PersistedTypeAndExtractor`
`.Tags`	A pointer to an instance of `bdTags` with information about the field's Go tags

And finally, for each member of `.FieldTypes`, we need to collect the following data. Note that because it is deduplicated metadata about `.Fields`, the definitions are identical.

Field	Description
`.IndexType`	The protobuf type to be used when indexing this type if `.IsIndexed`, blank otherwise
`.SanitizedType`	A string corresponding to `.IndexType` that can be safely included in the names of private functions

Walking the AST

Before we can walk the AST, let's set up some `structs` to collect the metadata described in the previous section. The most obvious one is for a single `struct` field:

```
// gen/lib/gen.go

type BdStructField struct {
  Name                    string
  ParamName               string
  TitleName               string
  ParamNameWithExtractor  string
  EDotNameWithExtractor   string
  Type                    string
  TransformedType         string
  IsPointer               bool
  IsContainer             bool
  IndexType               string
  SanitizedType           string
  IsBool                  bool
  CanIndex                bool
  mt                      *cshared.PersistedTypeAndExtractor
  Tags                    *bdTags
}
```

Note the use of `bdTags`, which describes the Go tags on a field:

```
// gen/lib/gen.go

type bdTags struct {
  IsIndexed bool
  IsKey     bool
  IsRef     bool
  IsRefs    bool
  RefsType  string
  IsUnique  bool
}
```

We'll omit the trivial constructor for `bdTags` and move on to the constructor for `BdStructField`. First, we'll make sure that the data is sane—that the type is persistable, that it can be indexed (if applicable), and so forth:

```
// gen/lib/gen.go

const (
  objectIdType        = "shared.ObjectId"
  objectIdTypeInTypeMap = "string"
)
```

```go
func NewBdStructField(
  name string,
  tipe string,
  isPointer bool,
  isContainer bool,
  tags *bdTags,
) *BdStructField {
  tipeInTypeMap := tipe
  if tipeInTypeMap == objectIdType {
    tipeInTypeMap = objectIdTypeInTypeMap
    isPointer = false
  } else if strings.Contains(tipeInTypeMap, ".") {
    a := strings.Split(tipeInTypeMap, ".")
    if unaliased, exists := importAliases[a[0]]; exists {
      a[0] = unaliased
    }
    tipeInTypeMap = strings.Join(a, ".")
  }
  var indexType string
  mt := cshared.GetFromTypeMap(tipeInTypeMap)
  if mt == nil && (tags.IsRef || tags.IsRefs) {
    mt = cshared.RefPersistedTypeAndExtractor
  }
  if tags.IsIndexed && mt == nil {
    log.Fatalf("Cannot persist %s of type %s", name, tipe)
  } else if tags.IsIndexed {
    indexType = strings.Title(mt.PersistedType.String())
    if !mt.CanIndex {
      log.Fatalf("Cannot index %s of type %s", name, tipe)
    }
  }
  if tags.IsRefs {
    tags.RefsType = tipe[3:]
  }
  ...
}
```

For the moment, it's enough to know that the `cshared.TypeMap` contains information for mapping from user types to database types and back, and we'll return to it in a moment. Continuing the constructor, all that remains is to return a populated `struct`:

```go
// gen/lib/gen.go

  ...
  sf := &BdStructField{
    Name:          name,
    ParamName:     NameToParamName(name),
    TitleName:     TitleizeName(name),
```

```
    Type:              tipe,
    TransformedType:  transformerFor(tipe),
    IsPointer:         isPointer,
    IsContainer:       isContainer,
    IndexType:         indexType,
    SanitizedType:     SanitizeType(indexType),
    IsBool:            tipe == "bool",
    Tags:              tags,
  }
  if mt != nil {
    sf.ParamNameWithExtractor = NameToParamName(name)
    sf.EDotNameWithExtractor = "e." + name
    if mt.Extractor != nil {
      sf.ParamNameWithExtractor =
        mt.Extractor(sf.ParamNameWithExtractor)
      sf.EDotNameWithExtractor =
        mt.Extractor(sf.EDotNameWithExtractor)
    }
    sf.CanIndex = mt.CanIndex
    sf.mt = mt
  }
  return sf
}
```

We'll need a few simple functions to fill that in:

```
// gen/lib/gen.go

const (
  bdTagIndex  = "index"
  bdTagKey    = "key"
  bdTagRef    = "ref"
  bdTagRefs   = "refs"
  bdTagUnique = "unique"
)

var (
  reDot = regexp.MustCompile(`\.`)
)

func NameToParamName(name string) string {
  return strings.ToLower(name[:1]) + name[1:]
}

func SanitizeType(tipe string) string {
  s := reDot.ReplaceAllLiteralString(tipe, "dot")
  s = strings.ToUpper(s[:1]) + s[1:]
  return s
}

func TitleizeName(name string) string {
```

```
  if name[:1] == "_" {
    name = name[1:]
  }
  name = strings.ToUpper(name[:1]) + name[1:]
  return name
}
```

We will leave `transformerFor` until later in the chapter.

Now, let's define a container for all of the fields held by a user's `struct`. Note that in `addField()`, we also keep track of the unique list of `.IndexedTypes` so that we can generate helper functions.

```go
// gen/lib/gen.go

type bdSanitizedTypeAndIndexType struct {
  SanitizedType      string
  IndexType          string
  ValueWithExtractor string
}

type BdStruct struct {
  Name       string
  Fields     []*BdStructField
  FieldTypes map[string]*bdSanitizedTypeAndIndexType
}

func NewBdStruct(name string) *BdStruct {
  return &BdStruct{
    Name:       name,
    Fields:     make([]*BdStructField, 0),
    FieldTypes: make(map[string]*bdSanitizedTypeAndIndexType),
  }
}
```

We'll also want to make it easy to add fields to `BdStruct`:

```go
// gen/lib/gen.go

func (b *BdStruct) AddField(
  name string, tipe string, isPointer bool, isContainer bool,
  isIndexed bool, isKey bool, isUnique bool,
  isRef bool, isRefs bool,
) {
  if isRef && isRefs {
    log.Fatal("Cannot set both isRef and isRefs for " + name)
  }
  fieldTipe := tipe
  b.Fields = append(b.Fields, NewBdStructField(
    name, fieldTipe, isPointer, isContainer,
```

```
    isIndexed, isKey, isUnique,
    isRef, isRefs))
  if isIndexed {
    if _, exists := b.FieldTypes[tipe]; !exists {
      v := "value"
      if e := b.Fields[len(b.Fields)-1].mt.Extractor; e != nil
{
        v = e(v)
      }
      b.FieldTypes[tipe] = &bdSanitizedTypeAndIndexType{
        SanitizedType:      SanitizeType(tipe),
        IndexType:          b.Fields[len(b.Fields)-
1].IndexType,
        ValueWithExtractor: v,
      }
    }
  }
}
```

And, we'll want to be able to process a `*ast.TypeSpec` into our `BdStruct`:

```
// gen/lib/gen.go

func (b *BdStruct) Process(structType *ast.StructType) {
  for _, field := range structType.Fields.List {
    if len(field.Names) == 0 {
      // This is an embedded struct.
      continue
    }
    fieldName := field.Names[0].Name
    fieldType, isPointer, isContainer := GetType(field)
    isIndexed := false
    isKey := false
    isUnique := false
    isRef := false
    isRefs := false
    if field.Tag != nil {
      tagValue := field.Tag.Value
      tag := reflect.StructTag(tagValue[1 : len(tagValue)-1])
      bdTag := tag.Get("bd")
      slog.Info("Tag", "tagValue", tagValue, "bdTag", bdTag)
      isIndexed = bdTag == bdTagIndex
      isKey = bdTag == bdTagKey
      isUnique = bdTag == bdTagUnique
      isRef = bdTag == bdTagRef
      isRefs = bdTag == bdTagRefs
      if !(isIndexed || isKey || isUnique || isRef || isRefs) {
        log.Fatalf("%s is not a valid tag", field.Tag)
      }
    }
    // isKey and isUnique imply isIndexed.
```

```
    isIndexed = isIndexed || isKey || isUnique
    b.AddField(fieldName, fieldType, isPointer, isContainer,
      isIndexed, isKey, isUnique, isRef, isRefs)
  }
}
```

That relies on `GetType()` to get both the type of the field and a `bool` indicating whether or not this is actually a reference (`isPointer`).

```
// gen/lib/gen.go

// Returns fieldType, isPointer, isContainer
func GetType(field *ast.Field) (string, bool, bool) {
  return GetTypeInner(field.Type, field.Names[0].Name)
}
```

Okay, that's not much of a function—it just calls `GetTypeInner()`. The reason to do so is that we want to pass a few extra pieces of data, and – as we'll see momentarily – we'll want to call `GetTypeInner()` recursively if we have a nested type.

```
// gen/lib/gen.go

// Returns fieldType, isPointer, isContainer
func GetTypeInner(
  fieldTypeExpr ast.Expr,
  structFieldName string,
) (string, bool, bool) {
  var fieldType string
  var isPointer bool
  var isContainer bool
  switch fieldTypeExpr.(type) {
  case *ast.Ident:
    fieldType = fieldTypeExpr.(*ast.Ident).Name
  case *ast.StarExpr:
    isPointer = true
    starExpr := fieldTypeExpr.(*ast.StarExpr)
    fieldType = getTypeInnerStarExpr(starExpr)
  case *ast.SelectorExpr:
    selExpr := fieldTypeExpr.(*ast.SelectorExpr)
    fieldType = getTypeInnerSelectorExpr(selExpr)
  case *ast.ArrayType:
    isContainer = true
    aTyp := fieldTypeExpr.(*ast.ArrayType)
    fieldType, _ /*isPointer*/ =
      getTypeInnerArrayType(aTyp, structFieldName)
  case *ast.MapType:
    isContainer = true
    mTyp := fieldTypeExpr.(*ast.MapType)
    fieldType, _ /*isPointer*/ =
```

```
      getTypeInnerMapType(mTyp, structFieldName)
  default:
    log.Fatalf(
      "Cannot generate for field %s of type %+v",
      structFieldName, fieldTypeExpr)
  }
  return fieldType, isPointer, isContainer
}
```

Then, we just fill in the cases:

```
// gen/lib/gen.go

func getTypeInnerStarExpr(
  starExpr *ast.StarExpr,
  structFieldName string,
) string {
  var fieldType string
  if i, ok := starExpr.X.(*ast.Ident); ok {
    fieldType = i.Name
  } else if selExpr, ok := starExpr.X.(*ast.SelectorExpr); ok {
    if i, ok := selExpr.X.(*ast.Ident); ok {
      fieldType = i.Name + "." + selExpr.Sel.Name
    } else {
      log.Fatalf("Failed to parse selExpr %+v on field %s",
        selExpr, structFieldName)
    }
  }
  if fieldType == "" {
    log.Fatalf("Failed to parse starExpr %+v on field %s",
      starExpr, structFieldName)
  }
  return fieldType
}
```

```
// gen/lib/gen.go

func getTypeInnerSelectorExpr(
  selExpr *ast.SelectorExpr,
  structFieldName string,
) string {
  var fieldType string
  didSet := false
  slog.Info("selExpr", "selExpr", selExpr, "X", selExpr.X)
  if _ /*i*/, ok := selExpr.X.(*ast.Ident); ok {
    fieldType = "string"
    didSet = true
  }
  if !didSet {
    log.Fatalf("Failed to parse SelectorExpr %+v on %s",
      selExpr, structFieldName)
```

```
  }
  return fieldType
}
```

```
// gen/lib/gen.go
```

```
func getTypeInnerArrayType(
  aTyp *ast.ArrayType,
  structFieldName string,
) (string, bool) {
  slog.Info("aTyp", "aTyp", aTyp, "Elt", aTyp.Elt)
  sel, isPointer, _ /* isContainer */ :=
    GetTypeInner(aTyp.Elt, structFieldName)
  if isPointer {
    sel = "*" + sel
  }
  return "[]" + sel, isPointer
}
```

```
// gen/lib/gen.go
```

```
func getTypeInnerMapType(
  mTyp *ast.MapType,
  structFieldName string,
) (string, bool) {
  slog.Info("mTyp", "mTyp", mTyp,
    "Key", mTyp.Key,
    "val", mTyp.Value)
  selKey, selKeyIsPointer, _ /* isContainer */ :=
    GetTypeInner(mTyp.Key, structFieldName)
  if selKeyIsPointer {
    selKey = "*" + selKey
  }
  selVal, selValIsPointer, _ /* isContainer */ :=
    GetTypeInner(mTyp.Value, structFieldName)
  if selValIsPointer {
    selVal = "*" + selVal
  }
  return "map[" + selKey + "]" + selVal, false
}
```

Recall that we might be generating code for multiple `struct`s from the same `infile`, so let's wrap them in a container, as well, along with `.PackageName`.

```
// gen/lib/gen.go
```

```
type BdTData struct {
  PackageName     string
  Structs         []*BdStruct
  IndexConditions map[string]string
}
```

```go
func NewBdTData(pkgName string) *BdTData {
  return &BdTData{
    PackageName: pkgName,
    IndexConditions: map[string]string{
      "Gt":  "GREATER_THAN",
      "Gte": "GREATER_THAN_OR_EQUAL_TO",
      "Lt":  "LESS_THAN",
      "Lte": "LESS_THAN_OR_EQUAL_TO",
    },
  }
}
```

We will need a way to add `structs` to that, too:

```go
// gen/lib/gen.go

func (b *BdTData) AddStruct(strct *BdStruct) {
  b.Structs = append(b.Structs, strct)
}
```

Now that we have some handy containers, let's look at the `main()` function. This is where we'll walk the AST and do most of the interesting work. Since this will run as a binary with no prior knowledge of the codebase, we start by collecting the `target`, the `infile`, and the `outfile`, which are the name of the `struct` for which we'll generate code, the name of the file where `target` is defined, and the name of the file that will be generated.

```go
// gen/main.go

func main() {
  var targetStructs gen.TargetStructsArray
  flag.Var(&targetStructs, "target",
    "name(s) of the struct(s) to generate")
  var infile string
  flag.StringVar(&infile, "infile", "",
    "name of the file to read")
  var outfile string
  flag.StringVar(&outfile, "outfile", "",
    "name of the file to write")
  flag.Parse()
  if len(targetStructs) == 0 {
    log.Fatal("No targets provided")
  }
  targetStructsM := make(map[string]struct{})
  for _, ts := range targetStructs {
    if ts == "" {
      log.Fatalf("Invalid target \"%s\"", ts)
    }
    targetStructsM[ts] = struct{}{}
```

```
  }
  if infile == "" {
    log.Fatal("No infile provided")
  } else if !strings.HasSuffix(infile, ".go") {
    log.Fatal(fmt.Sprintf("Invalid file %s", infile))
  }
  if outfile == "" {
    if strings.HasSuffix(infile, "_test.go") {
      re := regexp.MustCompile(`_test\.go$`)
      outfile = re.ReplaceAllLiteralString(infile,
"_gen_test.go")
    } else {
      re := regexp.MustCompile(`\.go$`)
      outfile = re.ReplaceAllLiteralString(infile, "_gen.go")
    }
  }
  ...
```

If all of the flags are okay, then we can remove the existing file, if it exists:

```
// gen/main.go

  ...
  if _, err := os.Stat(outfile); err == nil {
    err := os.Remove(outfile)
    if err != nil {
      log.Fatal(err)
    }
  } else if os.IsNotExist(err) {
    // Okay
  } else {
    log.Fatalf("Failed to check if file exists: %w", err)
  }
  ...
```

With that out of the way, we can parse the file:

```
// gen/main.go

  ...
  fset := token.NewFileSet()
  file, err := parser.ParseFile(
    fset, infile, nil, parser.AllErrors)
  if err != nil {
    log.Fatal(fmt.Sprintf(
      "Failed to parse %s: %s",
      infile, err.Error()))
  }
  slog.Info("Parsed", "infile", infile)

  gen.GenImportAliases(file)
```

```
slog.Info("Got import aliases", "infile", infile)
...
```

And finally, we can get to the interesting part. We'll start by creating a new `BdTData`. Then, for every top-level node in `infile`, we'll check whether or not it's a `GenDecl`, which is an import constant, type, or var. If it's a `TypeSpec`, which represents a type declaration, then we check whether or not it's one of the `struct`s in `targets`. If it is, then we check whether or not it's a `StructType`, which represents a `struct`. (Fortunately, the naming makes this pretty obvious.) As an error check, if it's not a `StructType`, then the `default` case is a fatal error informing the user that the given target is not a `struct`, so the generator cannot proceed.

Now that we know that we're working on a `struct` that the user requested, we iterate over `.Fields.List`, which is ... a list of the `struct`'s fields. First, if there are no `.Names`, then we know that we hit an embedded `struct`, and we can simply ignore it. Otherwise, we collect the name and other metadata. The most interesting part is in `.Tag`, which is a `BasicLit` representing what's in the struct tag. Suppose we have the following:

```
type Employee struct {
  First  string `json:"f"`
  Middle string `json:"m,omitempty"`
  Last   string `json:"l"`
}

var e = &Employee{"Alice", "Bianca", "Carson"}
```

The `json:"..."` annotations after each field are struct tags, and they are available for other code to inspect in order to change its own behavior. For example, without the tags, marshaling `e` above to JSON using the standard `encoding/json` library would produce `{"First":"Alice","Middle":"Bianca","Last":"Carson"}`. However, the first and third tags rename "First" to "f" and "Last" to "l", and the second tag both renames "Middle" to "m" and instructs the library to omit the field entirely if "Middle" is empty. With the tags, marshaling `e` above to JSON would produce `{"f":"Alice","m":"Bianca","l":"Carson"}`. We will use the same technique, struct tags, to allow users to mark fields as indexed (or other such annotations) using the syntax `bd:"index"`.

Back in the AST, if we spot a `bd:"index"` tag, we set `.IsIndexed = true` for that field. Finally, we add the field's metadata to the `struct`'s metadata, and after checking all fields, add the `struct`'s metadata to the container of all `struct`s.

```
// gen/main.go

...
```

```
tData := gen.NewBdTData(file.Name.Name)
for _, node := range file.Decls {
  switch node.(type) {
  case *ast.GenDecl:
    genDecl := node.(*ast.GenDecl)
    for _, spec := range genDecl.Specs {
      switch spec.(type) {
      case *ast.TypeSpec:
        typeSpec := spec.(*ast.TypeSpec)
        switch typeSpec.Type.(type) {
        case *ast.StructType:
          structName := typeSpec.Name.Name
          slog.Info("struct", "name", structName)
          if _, exists := targetStructsM[structName]; exists
{
            strct := gen.NewBdStruct(structName)
            structType := typeSpec.Type.(*ast.StructType)
            strct.Process(structType)
            tData.AddStruct(strct)
            slog.Info("Added", "structName", structName)
          }
        }
      }
    }
  }
}
...
```

Let's ensure that we have collected the expected number of structs:

```
// gen/main.go

  ...
  if len(tData.Structs) != len(targetStructsM) {
    collectedNames := make([]string, len(tData.Structs))
    for i, s := range tData.Structs {
      collectedNames[i] = s.Name
    }
    wantedNames := make([]string, len(targetStructsM))
    i := 0
    for s := range targetStructsM {
      wantedNames[i] = s
      i++
    }
    log.Fatalf("Wrong number of structs collected: %s vs %s",
      strings.Join(collectedNames, ","),
      strings.Join(wantedNames, ","))
  }
  ...
```

119

At this point, we have `TData` populated, so all we have to do is render the template and write it to `outfile`:

```
// gen/main.go

  ...
  t := template.Must(
    template.New("code").Parse(strings.TrimSpace(gen.Tmpl)))
  if _, err := os.Stat(outfile); err == nil {
    err := os.Remove(outfile)
    if err != nil {
      log.Fatal(err)
    }
  }
  f, err := os.OpenFile(outfile, os.O_RDWR|os.O_CREATE, 0644)
  if err != nil {
    log.Fatal(err)
  }
  err = t.Execute(f, tData)
  if err != nil {
    log.Fatal(err)
  }
  ...
```

And for good measure, we'll clean up the imports and format the code properly:

```
// gen/main.go

  ...
  cmd := exec.Command("goimports", "-w", outfile)
  err = cmd.Run()
  if err != nil {
    log.Fatal(err)
  }
  cmd = exec.Command("gofmt", "-w", "-s", "-l", outfile)
  err = cmd.Run()
  if err != nil {
    log.Fatal(err)
  }
}
```

With all that out of the way, let's return to `cshared.TypeMap`. It's not hard to imagine how we might persist, say, an `int32` in a JSON document. It's somewhat harder to imagine how we would persist, say, a `time.Time`, or any other non-primitive type. (Even `complex64`, `complex128`, and `error` require special treatment, as we noted earlier in the chapter.) This is where the `TypeMap` comes in handy. The `TypeMap` is the registry of necessary information to serialize and deserialize an arbitrary type using JSON. Let's first look at the `interface` for `PersistableField`:

```go
// client/shared/persistable_field.go

type PersistableField interface {
  MarshalJSON() ([]byte, error)
  UnmarshalJSON(data []byte) error
  Value() interface{}
}
```

To persist a `time.Time` as a field of a `struct`, we can use the following implementation:

```go
// client/shared/persistable_time.go

var _ PersistableField = &PersistableTime{}

// NB This does not track the time zone. Unmarshal always
returns UTC.
type PersistableTime struct {
  T time.Time
}

func NewPersistableTime(t time.Time) *PersistableTime {
  return &PersistableTime{t}
}

func (p *PersistableTime) MarshalJSON() ([]byte, error) {
  m, ok := p.Value().(int64)
  if !ok {
    return nil, fmt.Errorf(
      "Cannot convert %+v to int64", p.Value())
  }
  return json.Marshal(m)
}

func (p *PersistableTime) UnmarshalJSON(data []byte) error {
  var m int64
  if err := json.Unmarshal(data, &m); err != nil {
    return err
  }
  f := int64(1e6)
  seconds := m / f
  microseconds := m % f
  p.T = time.Unix(seconds, microseconds*1000).UTC()
  return nil
}

func (p *PersistableTime) Value() interface{} {
  return p.T.UnixMicro()
}
```

Once we have a new type such as `PersistableTime`, we need to register it with the `TypeMap`, which we'll do shortly. Let's first take a look at the structure of some built-in types:

```go
// client/shared/type_map.go

type PersistedType int8

const (
  Bool PersistedType = iota
  Bytes
  Int32
  Int64
  Uint32
  Uint64
  Float
  Double
  String
)

type PersistedTypeAndExtractor struct {
  PersistedType PersistedType
  CanIndex      bool
  Extractor     func(raw string) string
}
```

Each of the built-in `PersistedType`s has an associated `Extractor` that can produce the correct type for the runtime given the type from the backend:

```go
// client/shared/type_map.go

var (
  typeMap = map[string]*PersistedTypeAndExtractor{
    "bool": {Bool, true, nil},
    "byte": {Int32, true, func(r string) string {
      return "int32(" + r + ")"
    }},
    "complex64":  {Bytes, false, nil},
    "complex128": {Bytes, false, nil},
    "error":      {Bytes, false, nil},
    "float32":    {Float, true, nil},
    "float64":    {Double, true, nil},
    "int": {Int32, true, func(r string) string {
      return "int32(" + r + ")"
    }},
    "int8": {Int32, true, func(r string) string {
      return "int32(" + r + ")"
    }},
    "int16": {Int32, true, func(r string) string {
      return "int32(" + r + ")"
```

```
    }},
    "int32": {Int32, true, nil},
    "int64": {Int64, true, nil},
    "rune": {Int32, true, func(r string) string {
      return "int32(" + r + ")"
    }},
    "string": {String, true, nil},
    "uint8": {Uint32, true, func(r string) string {
      return "uint32(" + r + ")"
    }},
    "uint16": {Uint32, true, func(r string) string {
      return "uint32(" + r + ")"
    }},
    "uint32": {Uint32, true, nil},
    "uint64": {Uint64, true, nil},
  }
  RefPersistedTypeAndExtractor = &PersistedTypeAndExtractor{
    String, true, func(r string) string { return r },
  }
)
```

Finally, let's see how we can add entries, such as our `PersistableTime`:

```
// client/shared/type_map.go

func AddTypeMapEntry(
  localType string,
  canIndex bool,
  wireType PersistedType,
) {
  if x, exists := typeMap[localType]; exists {
    log.Default().Fatal("localType already exists",
      "localType", localType,
      "x.PersistedType", x.PersistedType)
  }
  pte := &PersistedTypeAndExtractor{
    PersistedType: wireType,
    CanIndex:      canIndex,
  }
  switch wireType {
  ...
  }
  typeMap[localType] = pte
}
```

Now, to fill in the cases:

```
// client/shared/type_map.go

  ...
  case Bool:
```

```
    pte.Extractor = func(r string) string {
      return r + ".Value().(bool)"
    }
  case Bytes:
    pte.Extractor = func(r string) string {
      return r + ".Value().([]byte)"
    }
  case Int32:
    pte.Extractor = func(r string) string {
      return r + ".Value().(int32)"
    }
  case Int64:
    pte.Extractor = func(r string) string {
      return r + ".Value().(int64)"
    }
  case Uint32:
    pte.Extractor = func(r string) string {
      return r + ".Value().(uint32)"
    }
  case Uint64:
    pte.Extractor = func(r string) string {
      return r + ".Value().(uint64)"
    }
  case Float:
    pte.Extractor = func(r string) string {
      return r + ".Value().(float32)"
    }
  case Double:
    pte.Extractor = func(r string) string {
      return r + ".Value().(float64)"
    }
  case String:
    pte.Extractor = func(r string) string {
      return r + ".Value().(string)"
    }
  default:
    log.Default().Fatal("Failed to build extractor",
      "wireType", wireType.String())
  ...
```

Now, we can call AddTypeMapEntry() for PersistableTime:

```
// client/shared/init.go

func init() {
  AddTypeMapEntry(
    "bitbucket.org/bradcater/bitemporal-book/"+
      "client/shared.PersistableTime",
    true,
    Int64)
}
```

We could follow the approach above for `PersistableComplex64`, `PersistableComplex128`, and `PersistableError` – that is, add those types to the `typeMap` so that users can persist them – and we do, although they are elided in the snippet above because the code is so repetitive. However, `complex64`, `complex128`, and `error` are built-in Go types; users shouldn't have to do anything special to use them in their models. Instead, we have the following bit of code to convert from Go's own types to our persistable types:

```
// gen/lib/transform_map.go

func transformerFor(n string) string {
  switch n {
  case "complex64":
    return "cshared.PersistableComplex64"
  case "complex128":
    return "cshared.PersistableComplex128"
  case "error":
    return "cshared.PersistableError"
  default:
    return ""
  }
}
```

That concludes the generator!

Chapter 11: Example

Now that we have a working bitemporal database, let's demonstrate its utility with an example.

Suppose that we run a bank that offers checking accounts and extends lines of credit. Each checking account has a non-negative balance representing the amount of money that the account owner has. Each line of credit has a non-negative balance representing the amount of money that the account owner owes and a positive interest rate representing the annual interest rate. Each account and each line of credit is owned by a single customer who is free to draw additional funds from the line of credit at any time, and we (the bank) charge interest on the first of each month on the outstanding balance. Here's how we might model these:

```go
// examples/bank/models/customer.go

var _ cshared.HasValidator = &Customer{}

type Customer struct {
  cshared.BdObject
  Id        int `bd:"key"`
  FirstName string
  LastName  string `bd:"index"`
  Email     string `bd:"unique"`
}

func (c *Customer) Validate() error {
  if len(strings.TrimSpace(c.FirstName)) == 0 {
    return fmt.Errorf("FirstName must not be blank")
  } else if len(strings.TrimSpace(c.LastName)) == 0 {
    return fmt.Errorf("LastName must not be blank")
  }
  _, err := mail.ParseAddress(c.Email)
  if err != nil {
    return fmt.Errorf("Email is invalid: %s", err.Error())
  }
  return nil
}

// examples/bank/models/checking_account.go

var _ cshared.HasValidator = &CheckingAccount{}

type CheckingAccount struct {
  cshared.BdObject
  Id        int          `bd:"key"`
  Balance   int          // In cents
  _customer *Customer    `bd:"ref"`
```

```
}

func (ca *CheckingAccount) Validate() error {
  if ca.Balance < 0 {
    return fmt.Errorf("Balance must be >= 0")
  } else if ca._customer == nil {
    return fmt.Errorf("_customer must not be nil")
  }
  return nil
}

// examples/bank/models/line_of_credit.go

var _ cshared.HasValidator = &LineOfCredit{}

type LineOfCredit struct {
  cshared.BdObject
  Id           int        `bd:"key"`
  Balance      int        // In cents
  InterestRate int        // In basis points
  _customer    *Customer  `bd:"ref"`
}

func (loc *LineOfCredit) Validate() error {
  if loc.Balance < 0 {
    return fmt.Errorf("Balance must be >= 0")
  } else if loc.InterestRate <= 0 {
    return fmt.Errorf("InterestRate must be > 0")
  } else if loc._customer == nil {
    return fmt.Errorf("_customer must not be nil")
  }
  return nil
}

// examples/bank/models/interest_charge.go

var _ cshared.HasValidator = &InterestCharge{}

type InterestCharge struct {
  cshared.BdObject
  Datetime     *cshared.PersistableTime
  Amount       int                       // In cents
  _lineOfCredit *LineOfCredit `bd:"ref"`
}

func (ic *InterestCharge) Validate() error {
  if ic.Datetime == nil {
    return fmt.Errorf("Datetime must not be nil")
  } else if ic._lineOfCredit == nil {
    return fmt.Errorf("_lineOfCredit must not be nil")
  }
```

```
    return nil
}
```

In order for `Customer`s to pay off their `LineOfCredit`s, we'll also need to model payments to a `LineOfCredit`. (Let's ignore the fact that at some point, a `Customer` must also make a deposit into a `CheckingAccount` in order to fund it.)

```go
// examples/bank/models/payment.go

var _ cshared.HasValidator = &Payment{}

type Payment struct {
  cshared.BdObject
  Datetime          *cshared.PersistableTime
  Amount            int
  _checkingAccount  *CheckingAccount `bd:"ref"`
  _lineOfCredit     *LineOfCredit    `bd:"ref"`
}

func (p *Payment) Validate() error {
  if p.Datetime == nil {
    return fmt.Errorf("Datetime must not be nil")
  } else if p.Amount <= 0 {
    return fmt.Errorf("Amount must be > 0")
  } else if p._checkingAccount == nil {
    return fmt.Errorf("_checkingAccount must not be nil")
  } else if p._lineOfCredit == nil {
    return fmt.Errorf("_lineOfCredit must not be nil")
  }
  return nil
}
```

Now, let's suppose that we have a `Customer` who obtains a `LineOfCredit` on January 2nd with a starting balance of $1,000. The `Customer` makes a `Payment` on February 28th without issue, then makes a `Payment` on March 31st that doesn't post until April 7th. We, the bank, add an `InterestCharge` on April 1st (in error!) on the money that the customer paid on time but that we didn't post (again, in error!) until 8 days later.

In order to fix this, we need to update the `InterestCharge` with vtFrom == April_1st, and we need to update the balance of the `LineOfCredit` accordingly. However, we also have to preserve the series of transactions that led us to make these corrections. We'll model this bitemporally. The sequence of actions is as follows:

Date	Action
Jan 1	Create `Customer`, `CheckingAccount`, and `LineOfCredit`
Feb 1	Create `InterestCharge` for Jan

Date	Action
Feb 28	Create `Payment` for Jan
Mar 1	Create `InterestCharge` for Feb
Apr 1	Create `InterestCharge` for Mar, not knowing about the Mar 31 payment
Apr 7	Create `Payment` for Feb with `vtFrom == Mar_31st`
Apr 7	Update the `InterestCharge` from Apr 1
Apr 7	Update the `LineOfCredit` balance to reflect the change

Although we have included a `Customer.Id` field, let's keep this example to a single `Customer` with `Id == 1`. Likewise, we'll limit the number of `CheckingAccounts` and `LineOfCredits` to one:

```
// examples/bank/bank.go

const (
  checkingAccountId = 1
  customerId        = 1
  lineOfCreditId    = 1
)
```

Next, let's define some helper functions. The first will be a combination of writing some objects and waiting for the `Lsqt` to catch up:

```
// examples/bank/bank.go

func putAndCatchUp(
  cli api.Client,
  vtFrom shared.Vt,
  os ...cshared.BdObjectI,
) shared.Tt {
  tt, err := cli.MultiPut(os, vtFrom)
  if err != nil {
    log.Fatal(err)
  }
  _, err = cli.CatchUp(tt, 5000)
  if err != nil {
    log.Fatal(err)
  }
  return tt
}
```

We will also want to make it easy to load the objects that we'll handle most often, which are `Customer`, `CheckingAccount`, and `LineOfCredit`:

```
// examples/bank/bank.go
```

```go
func loadCustomerPlus(
  cli api.Client,
  tc *shared.TemporalCoordinates,
) (*models.Customer,
  *models.CheckingAccount,
  *models.LineOfCredit,
) {
  custIt, err := cli.Get(
    models.NewCustomerQuery().IdEq(customerId).Build(), tc)
  if err != nil {
    log.Fatal(err)
  }
  cust := models.NewCustomerIterator(custIt).First()
  caIt, err := cli.Get(
    models.NewCheckingAccountQuery().CustomerEq(cust).Build(),
tc)
  if err != nil {
    log.Fatal(err)
  }
  ca := models.NewCheckingAccountIterator(caIt).First()
  locIt, err := cli.Get(
    models.NewLineOfCreditQuery().CustomerEq(cust).Build(), tc)
  if err != nil {
    log.Fatal(err)
  }
  loc := models.NewLineOfCreditIterator(locIt).First()
  return cust, ca, loc
}
```

Finally, let's set up a logging function so that we can see the state of the
LineOfCredit over time:

```go
// examples/bank/bank.go

const (
  timeFmt = "2006-01-02 15:04:05"
)

func logLinesOfCredit(
  cli api.Client,
  tc *shared.TemporalCoordinates,
) {
  custIt, err := cli.Get(
    models.NewCustomerQuery().IdEq(customerId).Build(), tc)
  if err != nil {
    log.Fatal(err)
  }
  cust := models.NewCustomerIterator(custIt).First()
  locIt, err := cli.Get(
    models.NewLineOfCreditQuery().CustomerEq(cust).Build(), tc)
  if err != nil {
```

```
      log.Fatal(err)
  }
  for _, loc := range models.NewLineOfCreditIterator(locIt).
    Items() {
    slog.Info("LineOfCredit",
      "Customer", cust.Id,
      "Balance", loc.Balance,
      "InterestRate", loc.InterestRate,
      "Tt", loc.TtResolvedAt().Time().UTC().
        Format(timeFmt),
      "Vt", loc.VtResolvedAt().Time().UTC().
        Format(timeFmt))
  }
}
```

From there, it's a simple matter of going step-by-step through the actions in the table above. Note that we'll use `MultiPut`so that writes to multiple objects, such as creating an `InterestCharge` and updating the balance of the `LineOfCredit`, are made transactionally.

As with every application using our database, we start by setting up a `Client`:

```
// examples/bank/bank.go

func main() {
  ctx := context.Background()
  cli := impl.NewClient(ctx)
  cli.Start()

  ...
}
```

Next, let's create the initial objects:

```
// examples/bank/bank.go

  ...
  slog.Info("Jan 1  | Create Customer, CheckingAccount, " +
    "LineOfCredit, and Withdrawal")
  cust := models.NewCustomer(
    customerId, "Alex", "Bank", "abank@bankers.com")
  initialCaBalance := 500 * 100 // $500 in cents
  ca := models.NewCheckingAccount(
    checkingAccountId, initialCaBalance, cust)
  initialLocBalance := 1000 * 100 // $1,000 in cents
  loc := models.NewLineOfCredit(
    lineOfCreditId, initialLocBalance, 590 /* 5.9% */, cust)
  wd := models.NewWithdrawal(initialLocBalance, cust, loc)
  vtFrom := shared.VtOf(
    time.Date(2000, time.January, 1, 0, 0, 0, 0, time.UTC))
```

```
tt := putAndCatchUp(cli, vtFrom, cust, ca, loc, wd)
logLinesOfCredit(cli, shared.NewTemporalCoordinates(tt,
vtFrom))
  ...
}
```

If you were to run this snippet, you would see something like this:

```
INFO Jan 1  | Create Customer, CheckingAccount, LineOfCredit, \
    and Withdrawal
INFO LineOfCredit Customer=1 Balance=100000 InterestRate=590 \
    Tt="2024-12-28 23:49:01" Vt="2000-01-01 00:00:00"
```

So far, so good: we have a Customer with `Id == 1` who has a `LineOfCredit` with a balance of $1,000 and an interest rate of 5.9%. (Your `Tt` will be different because your system clock is not synced with mine, but that doesn't change the relevant information.)

Now, let's create the January `InterestCharge`:

```
// examples/bank/bank.go

  ...
  slog.Info("Feb 1  | Create InterestCharge for Jan")
  t := time.Date(2000, time.February, 1, 0, 0, 0, 0, time.UTC)
  vtFrom = shared.VtOf(t)
  cust, _ /* ca */, loc = loadCustomerPlus(
    cli, shared.NewTemporalCoordinates(tt, vtFrom))
  accruedInterest :=
    loc.AccruedInterestForDays(31 /* 31 days in January */)
  slog.Info("InterestCharge", "accruedInterest",
accruedInterest)
  ic := models.NewInterestCharge(
    cshared.NewPersistableTime(t), accruedInterest, loc)
  loc.Balance += accruedInterest
  tt = putAndCatchUp(cli, vtFrom, ic, loc)
  logLinesOfCredit(cli, shared.NewTemporalCoordinates(tt,
vtFrom))
  ...
```

If you re-run the example, you'll find some new information logged:

```
INFO Feb 1  | Create InterestCharge for Jan
INFO AccruedInterestForDays loc.Balance=100000 days=31 i=501
INFO InterestCharge accruedInterest=501
INFO LineOfCredit Customer=1 Balance=100501 InterestRate=590 \
    Tt="2024-12-28 23:56:59" Vt="2000-02-01 00:00:00"
```

Let's create the `Payment` for January:

```
// examples/bank/bank.go
```

```
...
slog.Info("Feb 28 | Create Payment for Jan")
slog.Info("Payment", "amount", accruedInterest)
cust, ca, loc = loadCustomerPlus(
  cli, shared.NewTemporalCoordinates(tt, vtFrom))
t = time.Date(2000, time.February, 28, 0, 0, 0, 0, time.UTC)
p := models.NewPayment(
  cshared.NewPersistableTime(t), accruedInterest, ca, loc)
vtFrom = shared.VtOf(t)
ca.Balance -= p.Amount
loc.Balance -= p.Amount
tt = putAndCatchUp(cli, vtFrom, p, ca, loc)
logLinesOfCredit(cli, shared.NewTemporalCoordinates(tt,
vtFrom))
...
```

As expected, the `Customer` pays $5.01, and `LineOfCredit.Balance` is back down to $1,000:

```
INFO Feb 28 | Create Payment for Jan
INFO Payment amount=501
INFO LineOfCredit Customer=1 Balance=100000 InterestRate=590 \
    Tt="2024-12-28 23:59:16" Vt="2000-02-28 00:00:00"
```

On March 1, let's create the `InterestCharge` for February:

```
// examples/bank/bank.go

  ...
  slog.Info("Mar 1  | Create InterestCharge for Feb")
  t = time.Date(2000, time.March, 1, 0, 0, 0, 0, time.UTC)
  vtFrom = shared.VtOf(t)
  vtMar1 := vtFrom
  cust, ca, loc = loadCustomerPlus(
    cli, shared.NewTemporalCoordinates(tt, vtFrom))
  accruedInterest =
    loc.AccruedInterestForDays(29 /* 29 days in February, 2000
*/)
  slog.Info("InterestCharge", "accruedInterest",
accruedInterest)
  ic = models.NewInterestCharge(
    cshared.NewPersistableTime(t), accruedInterest, loc)
  loc.Balance += accruedInterest
  tt = putAndCatchUp(cli, vtFrom, ic, loc)
  logLinesOfCredit(cli, shared.NewTemporalCoordinates(tt,
vtFrom))
  ...
```

Here's the new output:

```
INFO Mar 1  | Create InterestCharge for Feb
INFO AccruedInterestForDays loc.Balance=100000 days=29 i=469
```

```
INFO InterestCharge accruedInterest=469
INFO LineOfCredit Customer=1 Balance=100469 InterestRate=590 \
    Tt="2024-12-29 00:05:54" Vt="2000-03-01 00:00:00"
```

On April 1, we create the `InterestCharge` for March, not knowing about the prior `Payment` on March 31:

```
// examples/bank/bank.go

  ...
  slog.Info("Apr 1  | Create InterestCharge for Mar, " +
    "not knowing about the Mar 31 Payment")
  t = time.Date(2000, time.April, 1, 0, 0, 0, 0, time.UTC)
  vtFrom = shared.VtOf(t)
  cust, ca, loc = loadCustomerPlus(
    cli, shared.NewTemporalCoordinates(tt, vtFrom))
  accruedInterest =
    loc.AccruedInterestForDays(31 /* 31 days in March */)
  slog.Info("InterestCharge", "accruedInterest",
accruedInterest)
  ic = models.NewInterestCharge(
    cshared.NewPersistableTime(t), accruedInterest, loc)
  loc.Balance += accruedInterest
  tt = putAndCatchUp(cli, vtFrom, ic, loc)
  logLinesOfCredit(cli, shared.NewTemporalCoordinates(tt,
vtFrom))
  ...
```

This produces:

```
INFO Apr 1  | Create InterestCharge for Mar, \
    not knowing about the Mar 31 Payment
INFO AccruedInterestForDays loc.Balance=100469 days=31 i=503
INFO InterestCharge accruedInterest=503
INFO LineOfCredit Customer=1 Balance=100972 InterestRate=590 \
    Tt="2024-12-29 00:11:23" Vt="2000-04-01 00:00:00"
```

Now create the `Payment` on March 31 with the amount of interest that was owed after the 29-day month of February, 2000:

```
// examples/bank/bank.go

  ...
  slog.Info("Mar 31 | Create Payment for Feb, but it's " +
    "received late, so it doesn't post until April 7. To " +
    "simulate this, we insert it after the InterestCharge " +
    "on Apr 1 but with only 29 days of interest.")
  priorAccruedInterest :=
    loc.AccruedInterestForDays(29 /* 29 days in February, 2000
*/)
  slog.Info("Payment", "amount", priorAccruedInterest)
  cust, ca, loc = loadCustomerPlus(
```

```
  cli, shared.NewTemporalCoordinates(tt, vtFrom))
t = time.Date(2000, time.March, 31, 0, 0, 0, 0, time.UTC)
p = models.NewPayment(
  cshared.NewPersistableTime(t), priorAccruedInterest, ca,
loc)
ca.Balance -= p.Amount
loc.Balance -= p.Amount
vtFrom = shared.VtOf(t)
tt = putAndCatchUp(cli, vtFrom, p, ca, loc)
logLinesOfCredit(cli, shared.NewTemporalCoordinates(tt,
vtFrom))
vtFrom = shared.VtOf(
  time.Date(2000, time.April, 1, 0, 0, 0, 0, time.UTC))
logLinesOfCredit(cli, shared.NewTemporalCoordinates(tt,
vtFrom))
...
```

And the new output:

```
INFO Mar 31 | Create Payment for Feb, but it's received late, \
    so it doesn't post until April 7. To simulate this, we \
    insert it after the InterestCharge on Apr 1 but with only \
    29 days of interest.
INFO AccruedInterestForDays loc.Balance=100972 days=29 i=473
INFO Payment amount=473
INFO LineOfCredit Customer=1 Balance=100499 InterestRate=590 \
    Tt="2024-12-29 00:29:10" Vt="2000-03-31 00:00:00"
INFO LineOfCredit Customer=1 Balance=100972 InterestRate=590 \
    Tt="2024-12-29 00:29:10" Vt="2000-04-01 00:00:00"
```

Finally, update the `InterestCharge` **and the** `LineOfCredit`**:**

```
// examples/bank/bank.go

  ...
  slog.Info("Apr 7  | Update the interest charged in error, " +
    "and update the LineOfCredit balance to reflect the
change.")
  vtFrom = shared.VtOf(
    time.Date(2000, time.March, 31, 0, 0, 0, 0, time.UTC))
  tc := shared.NewTemporalCoordinates(tt, vtMar1)
  _ /*cust*/, ca, loc = loadCustomerPlus(cli, tc)
  icIt, err := cli.Get(

models.NewInterestChargeQuery().LineOfCreditEq(loc).Build(),
    tc)
  ic = nil
  if err != nil {
    log.Fatal(err)
  }
  for _, x := range models.NewInterestChargeIterator(icIt).
    Items() {
```

```
    if !x.VtFrom().Equal(tc.Vt) {
      continue
    }
    if ic != nil {
      log.Fatal(
        fmt.Errorf("Did not expect more than one
InterestCharge"))
    }
    ic = x
  }
  ca.Balance += p.Amount
  loc.Balance -= p.Amount
  ic.Amount = loc.AccruedInterestForDays(31 /* 31 days in March
*/)
  vtFrom = shared.VtOf(
    time.Date(2000, time.April, 7, 0, 0, 0, 0, time.UTC))
  ca.Balance -= ic.Amount
  loc.Balance += ic.Amount
  tt = putAndCatchUp(cli, vtFrom, ic, ca, loc)
  logLinesOfCredit(cli, shared.NewTemporalCoordinates(tt,
vtFrom))
}
```

The final lines of output should be as follows:

```
INFO Apr 7  | Update the interest charged in error, and \
    update the LineOfCredit balance to reflect the change.
INFO AccruedInterestForDays loc.Balance=99996 days=31 i=501
INFO LineOfCredit Customer=1 Balance=100497 InterestRate=590 \
    Tt="2024-12-29 00:33:28" Vt="2000-04-07 00:00:00"
```

By using bitemporal principles we have preserved the complete history of
transactions for this customer.

www.ingramcontent.com/pod-product-compliance
Lightning Source LLC
LaVergne TN
LVHW080117070326
832902LV00015B/2642